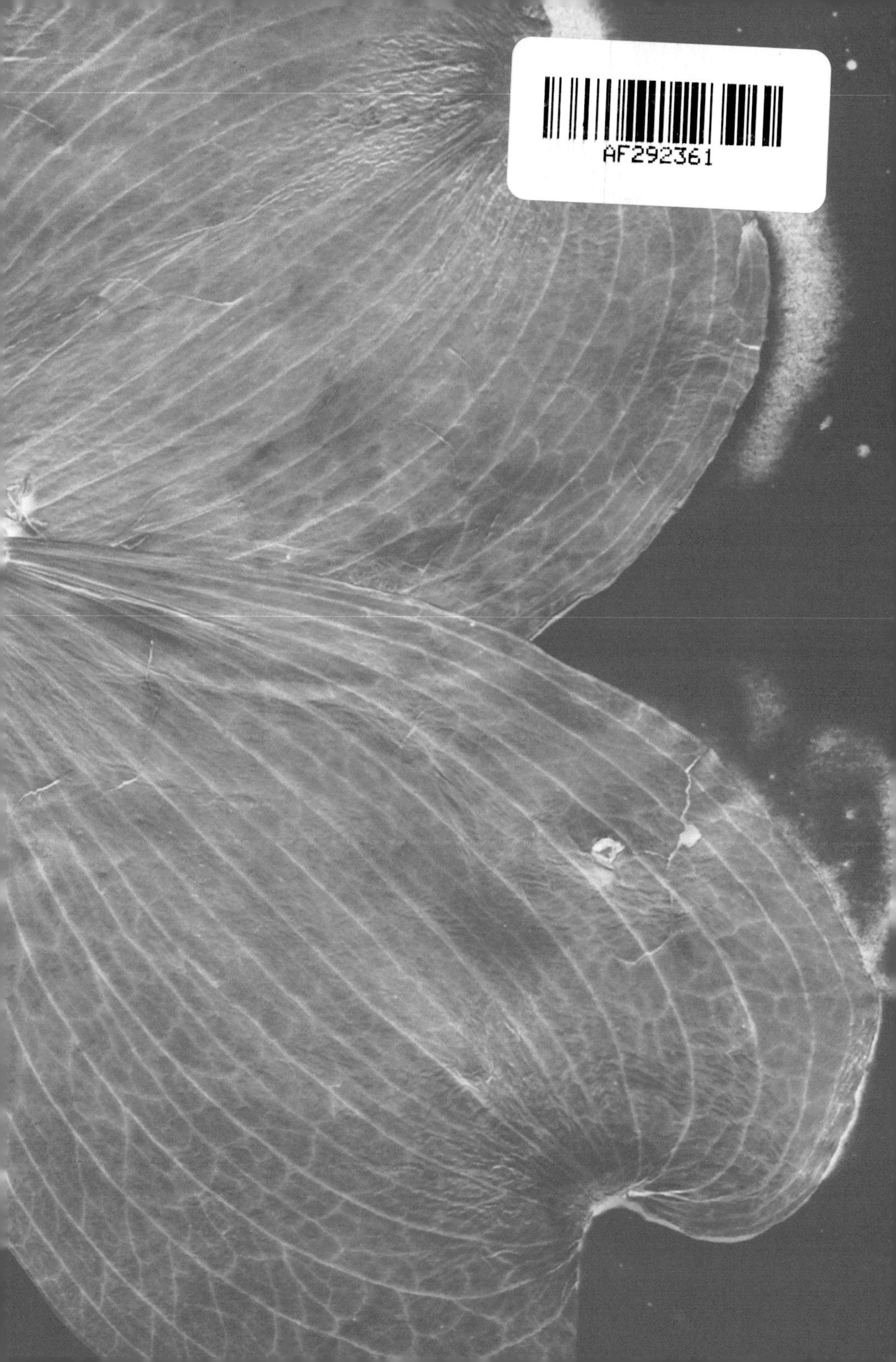
AF292361

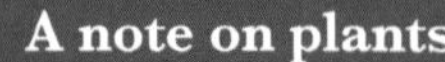

The visual material contained within this publication comes from the Smithsonian Institution's Open Access digital catalog. The images are from various institutions' herbaria and fall under Creative Commons usage.

The plants included here correspond to those contained in the artist's book, *A Tree Grows in Queens*, as well as trees to be found in and around the cities of New York and New Orleans where this book was originally printed on the occasion of the exhibition, *A Tree, A Garden* at Antenna.

The text is a loosely linked introduction and reflection upon the place of herbaria in historical and contemporary contexts.

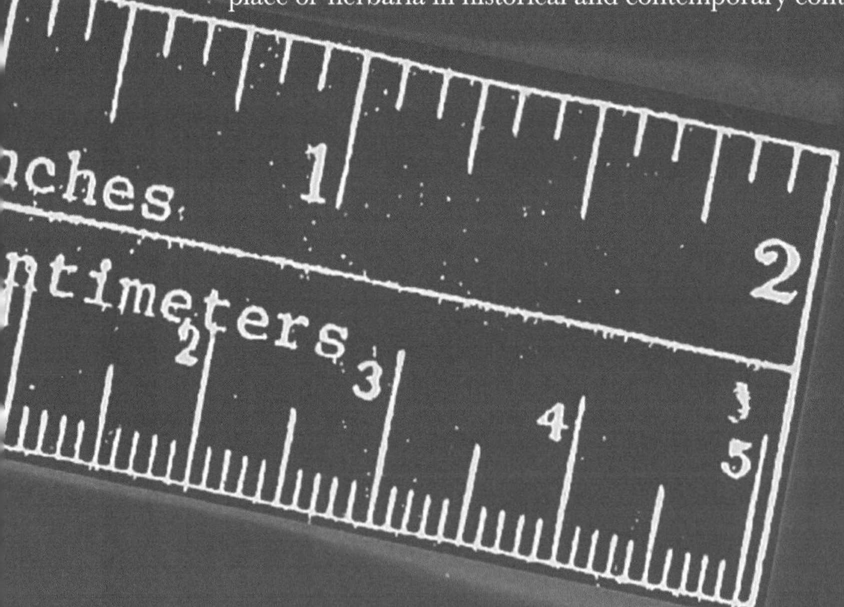

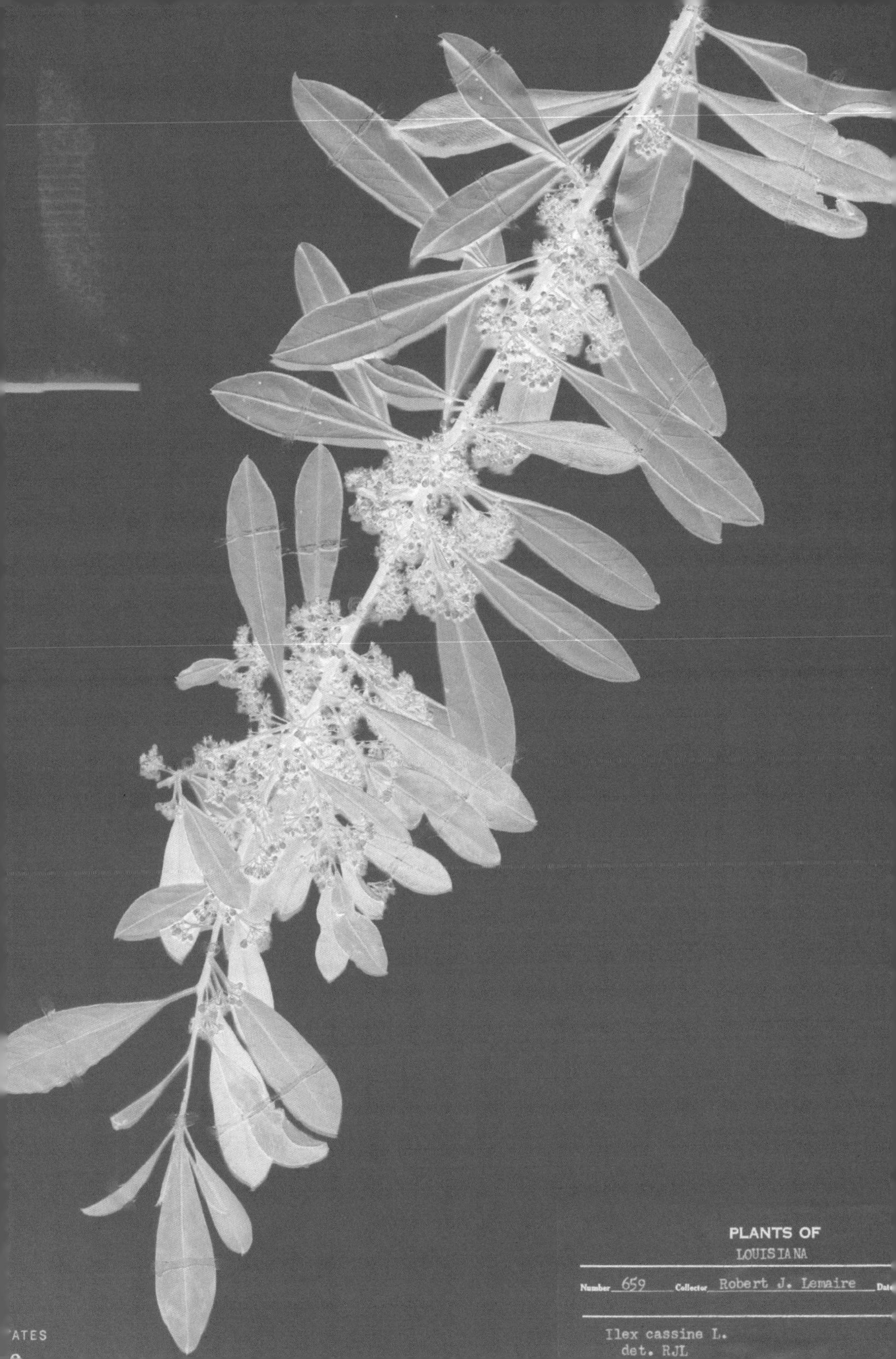
PLANTS OF
LOUISIANA
Number 659   Collector Robert J. Lemaire   Date
Ilex cassine L.
det. RJL
ATES

Blue from Red

The layout of this book is inspired by one of the first photographic books ever published. In 1843, Anna Atkins, a British botanist and photographer, privately published *British Algae: Cyanotype Impressions.* Using the new medium of cyanotype photography, Atkins' album featured pages of delicate white fronds and limbs floating in a sea of blue. She explained her novel pursuit as an effort "to obtain impressions of plants themselves."[1] Over a decade, Atkins would produce three volumes of seaweed images. Alongside her childhood friend Anne Dixon she would create three more volumes of images depicting ferns and pressed flowers (as well as a book entitled, *Murder will out. A story of real life*).[2] In 1842, Sir John Herschel, a polymath who pursued astronomy, botany, mathematics, and chemistry, invented the cyanotype process using ammonium ferric citrate and potassium ferricyanide. A deep Prussian blue image would appear when objects were placed upon the treated surface and exposed to UV light. Prussian blue, the first synthetic blue pigment, was most likely first created by mistake when a painter, attempting to create a red dye from cochineal, a type of insect, used contaminated potash. The cyanotype would become the process for creating architectural blueprints, a cheap, simple means of reproduction.

---

1. Atkins, Anna. *British Algae: Cyanotype Impressions* (Self-published) 1843.

2. Lotzof, Kerry. *Anna Atkins's Cyantoypes*
https://www.nhm.ac.uk/discover/anna-atkins-cyano-types-the-first-book-of-photographs.html

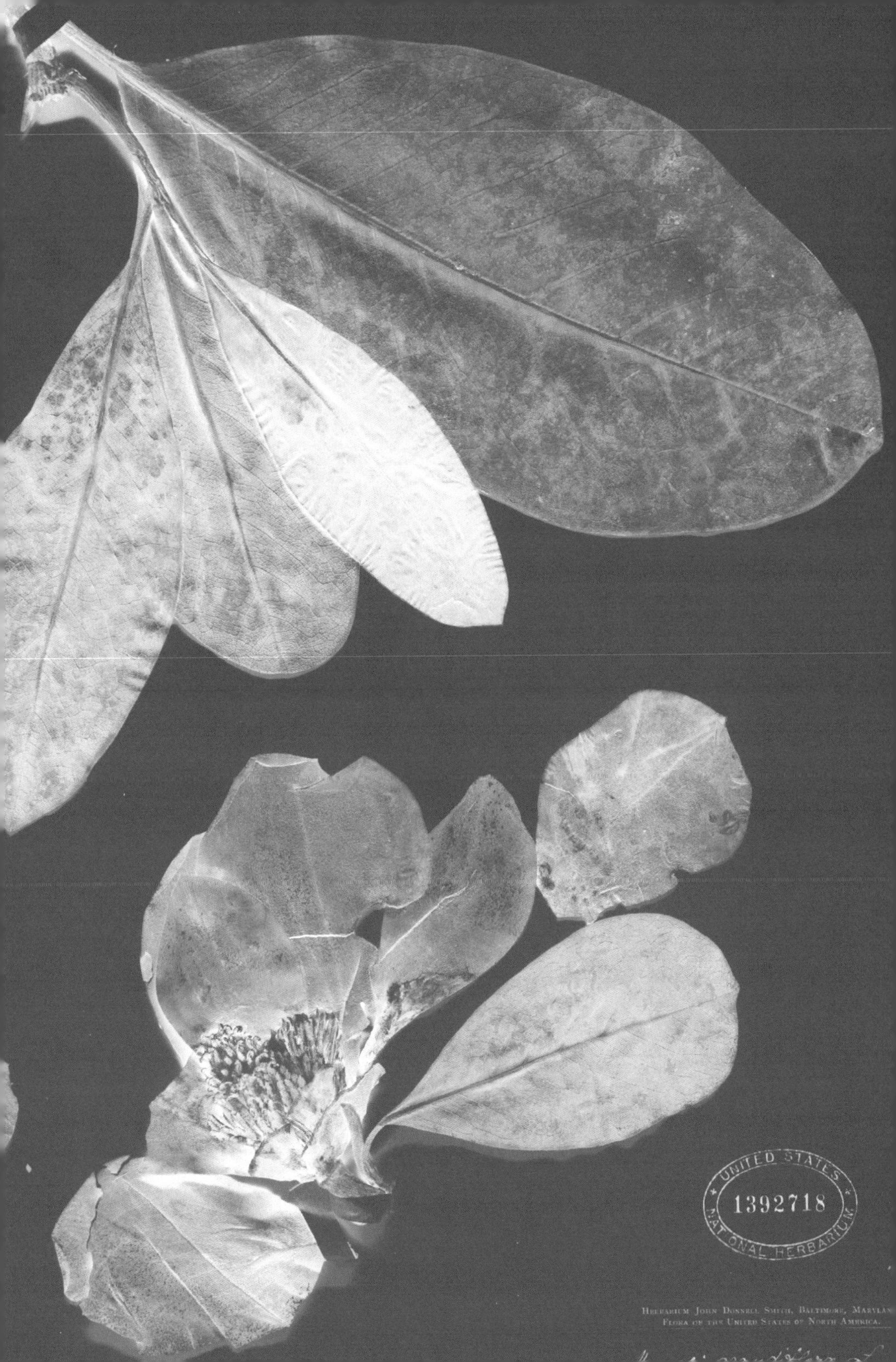

UNITED STATES
1392718
NATIONAL HERBARIUM

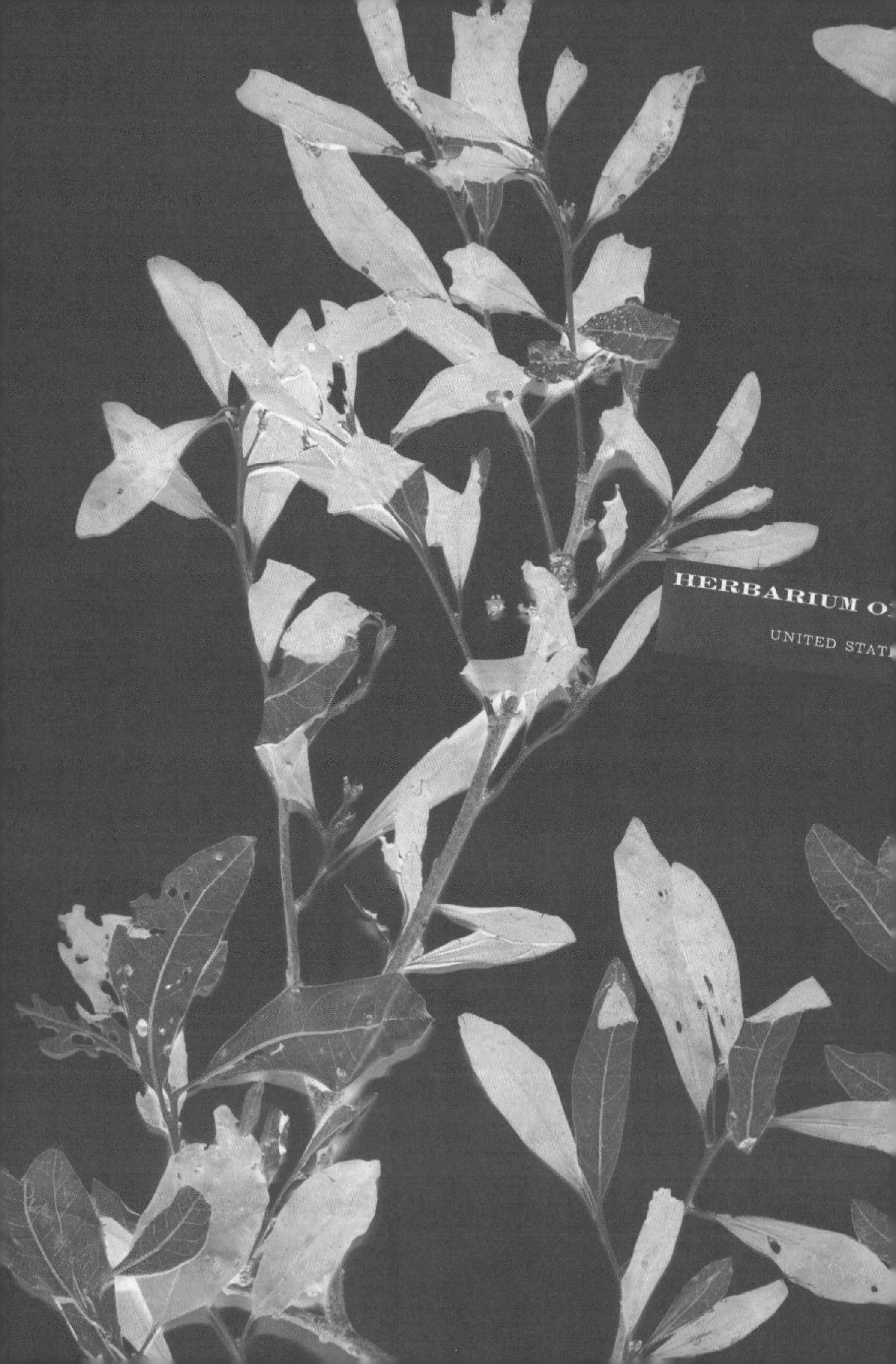

HERBARIUM OF
UNITED STAT

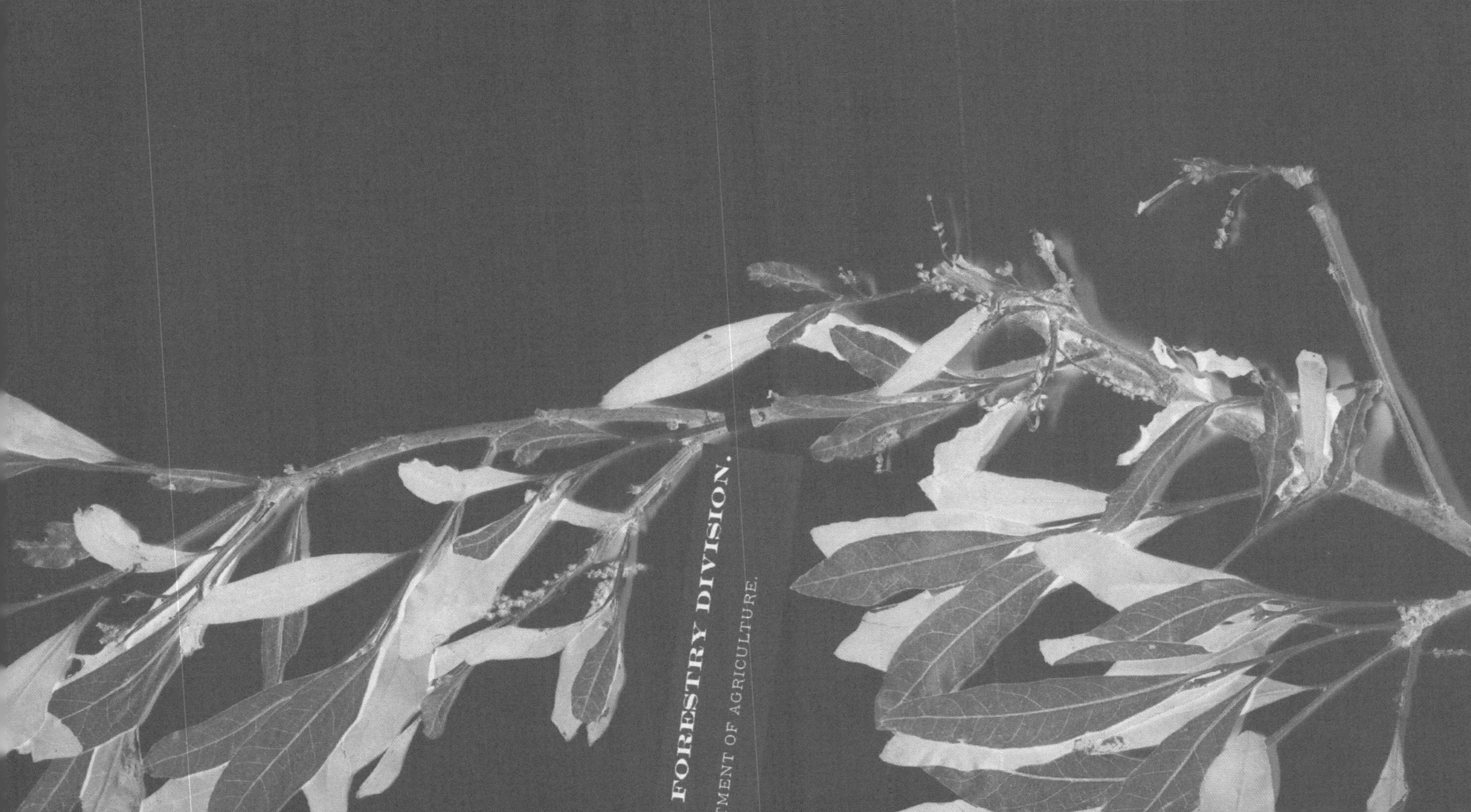
Golden Thread
Colors by Munsell Color Services Lab
Smithsonian Institution
US
FORESTRY DIVISION.
DEPARTMENT OF AGRICULTURE.

I. *Hortus Siccus* : **Dry Garden**
A Brief History

Standing in the basement level etymological collection, my eye catches on a slim beige book with two dainty black ribbons to keep it closed. There is something wonderfully delicate about it, surrounded by the clinical wall of white cabinets wheeled apart to reveal tray after tray of insect specimens. In softly accented English, the curator holds up a glass-fronted wooden box and explains that the miniscule specimens are moths gathered by an amateur collector (a black-and-white photographic portrait is proffered depicting a serious looking man with a mustache as thick as a scrub brush). The curator pulls out the beige book, untying the black ribbons to reveal it as the collector's herbarium. For each moth labeled, he also included the plant he found them on. Pressed, pasted down, and notated. The herbarium contains the collection date, weather conditions, the moth's habitat, and even the silky sac it laid eggs in. Page after page of dried plants accompanied by spidery, meticulous handwriting between the covers.

Herbariums are old-fashioned and yet immensely useful today. A herbarium is a collection of dried plant specimens used in many diverse scientific fields of study. The Latin suffix *-arium* refers to a place where something is stored or located, *-herba* means herbs or vegetation. They have informed research on the geographic distribution of plant life, taxonomy (the naming and identifying of plants), climate change, seed study, species migration, and provided DNA samples for genetic mapping. Herbaria have many collection relations from fungarium for fungi, hortorium for horticultural studies, and xylarium for collections of tree bark. Classifying, organizing, and systemizing, all forms of the deeply human trait of figuring.

In a video by the Royal Botanic Garden of Edinburgh, Deputy Curator Elspeth Haston calls the herbarium pages spread in front of her "a point in space and time."[1] Each one provides a collection date and place. Characteristics such as color, texture and habitat are marked down, roots, stems, leaves and flowers are pressed into the paper. They are stored as single sheets, leading them to be called "hanging gardens."

The first herbarium, referred to as a *hortus siccus* (dry garden), is said to have been created by the Italian botanist Luca Ghini, who is also credited as the founder of the first European university botanical garden in Pisa in 1544.[2] His radical idea was that studying dried specimens would be more beneficial than attempting to decipher plant descriptions from ancient texts.

Up until this point, most botanists and physicians used the ancient Greek *De Materia Medica*, a pharmacopeia or herbal of medicinal plants that was in use for over 1500 years. The *Materia Medica* was translated into Latin and Arabic. It identified many plants still in use today, from aloe as a soothing gel, calamine to ease itching, and willow as a painkiller (which would later make its way into aspirin). Herbals were found worldwide including in ancient Egypt, China, and India. The *Shennong Bencao Jing*, the first Chinese herbal, is said to have been composed in 2700 BCE. An Aztec herbal, *Libellus de Medicinalibus Indorum Herbis* (its Latin translation), written originally in the Nahuatl language dates from 1552. It offered cures against "stupidity of the mind" and the "goaty armpits of sick people." With the advent of the printing press, herbals flourished throughout Europe before being replaced with more scientific texts in the Age of Enlightenment. Joseph Pitton de Tournefort, a French botanist, was the first to use the word herbarium to replace the term *hortus siccus* (or sometimes *hortus mortus*, dead garden). Before this, herbarium was used exclusively for collections that focused on the medicinal use of plants.

The collecting of live plants has an even longer history. A quick Wikipedia search notes a Chinese botanist collecting roses 5000 years ago and Queen Hatshepsut, the fifth pharaoh of Egypt's Eighteenth Dynasty, sending collectors to Somalia to bring back incense trees (to produce frankincense) in 1495 BC. Fads of live plant collecting have bubbled up over the years. During the Dutch Golden Age, the buying and selling of tulips reached a fever pitch and led to what is considered the first financial speculative bubble. Prices for single bulbs rose to nearly ten times the income of craftspeople and then spectacularly collapsed. *Pteridomania*, aka fern fever, and *Orchidelirium*, gripped Victorians and almost led to the extinction of certain rare varieties. Not all collecting was quite so destructive, but plant collecting, in all its forms, has gripped the imagination for millennia.

Of course, the herbarium is a bit different. Unlike the Victorian hobbyist collectors, armed with forerunners to sticker books in which some plants were already included, botanists were looking to something larger — to make sense of the world.

---

1. https://www.rbge.org.uk/science-and-conservation/herbarium/

2. Vardi, Sarai. "A Brief History of Plants in Books" Royal Botanic Garden at Kew https://www.kew.org/read-and-watch/a-brief-history-of-plants-in-book

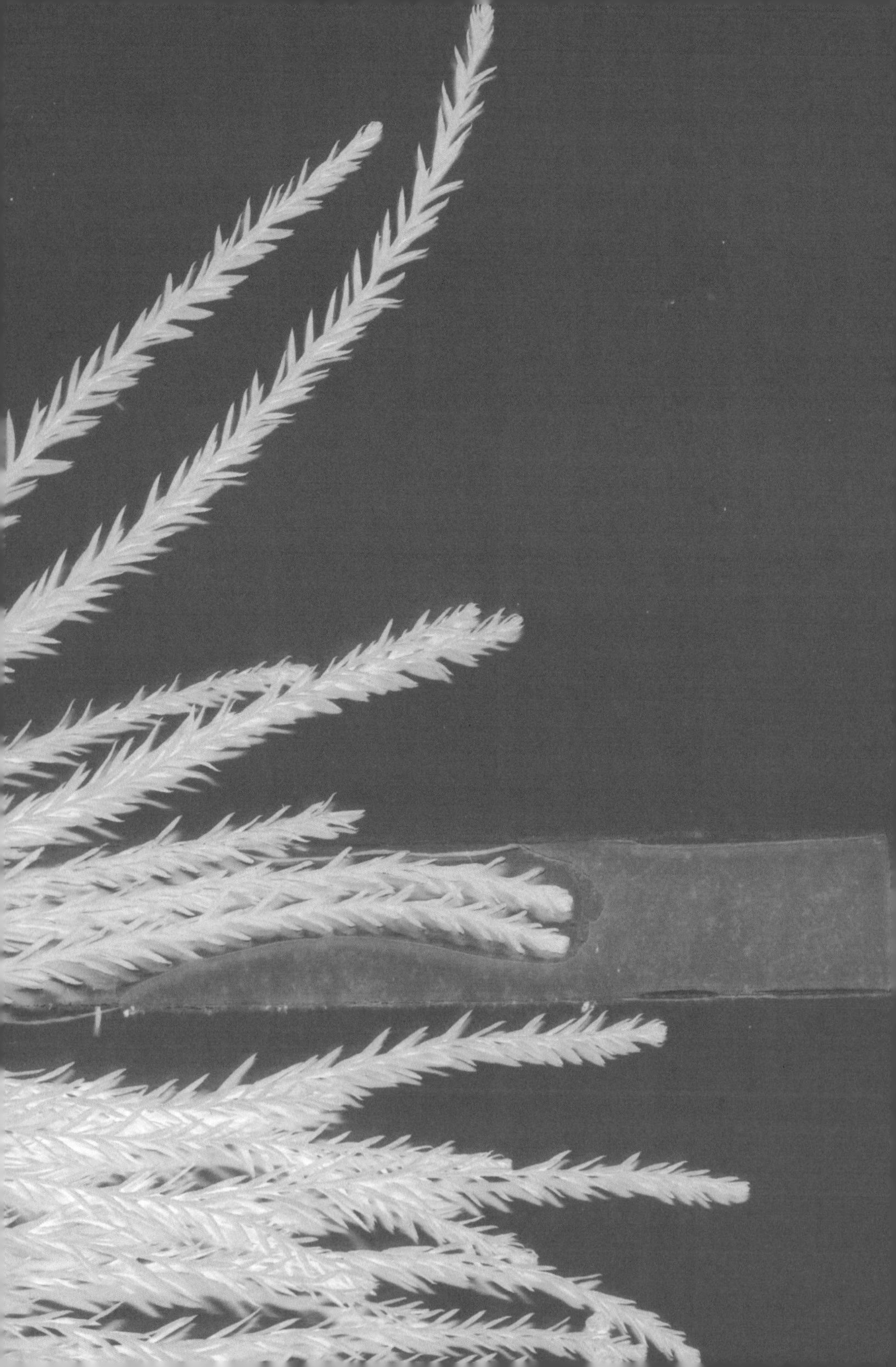

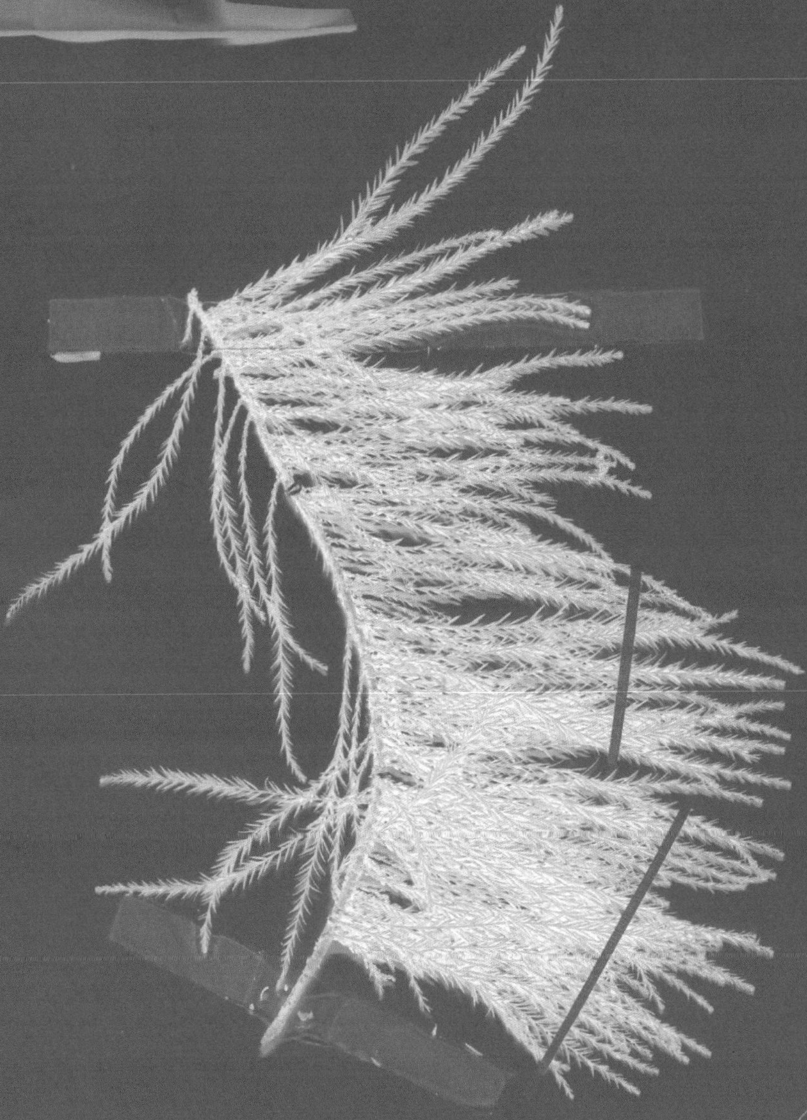

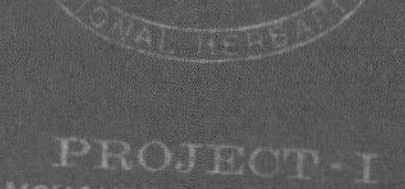

PROJECT-I
VOUCHER-MATERIAL FOR
WOOD SAMPLES

THE NEW YORK STATE COLLEGE OF FORESTRY
DENDROLOGY AND WOOD TECHNOLOGY

No. 8149   Date 7/8/35

Sci. Name Taxodium distichum (L) Richa.

Common Name Bald Cypress

Habitat Swamp   Locality Urania, La

Image No.

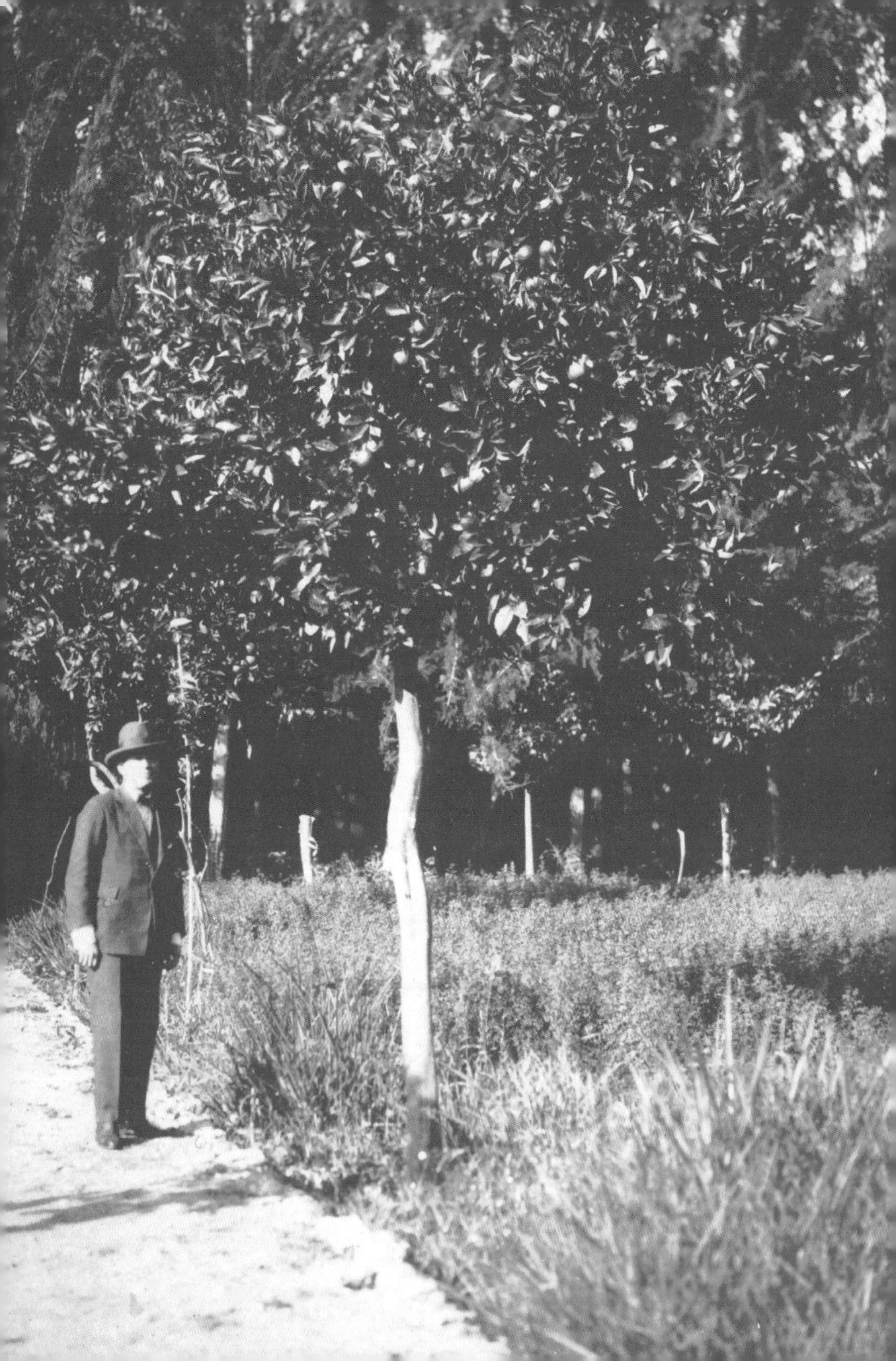

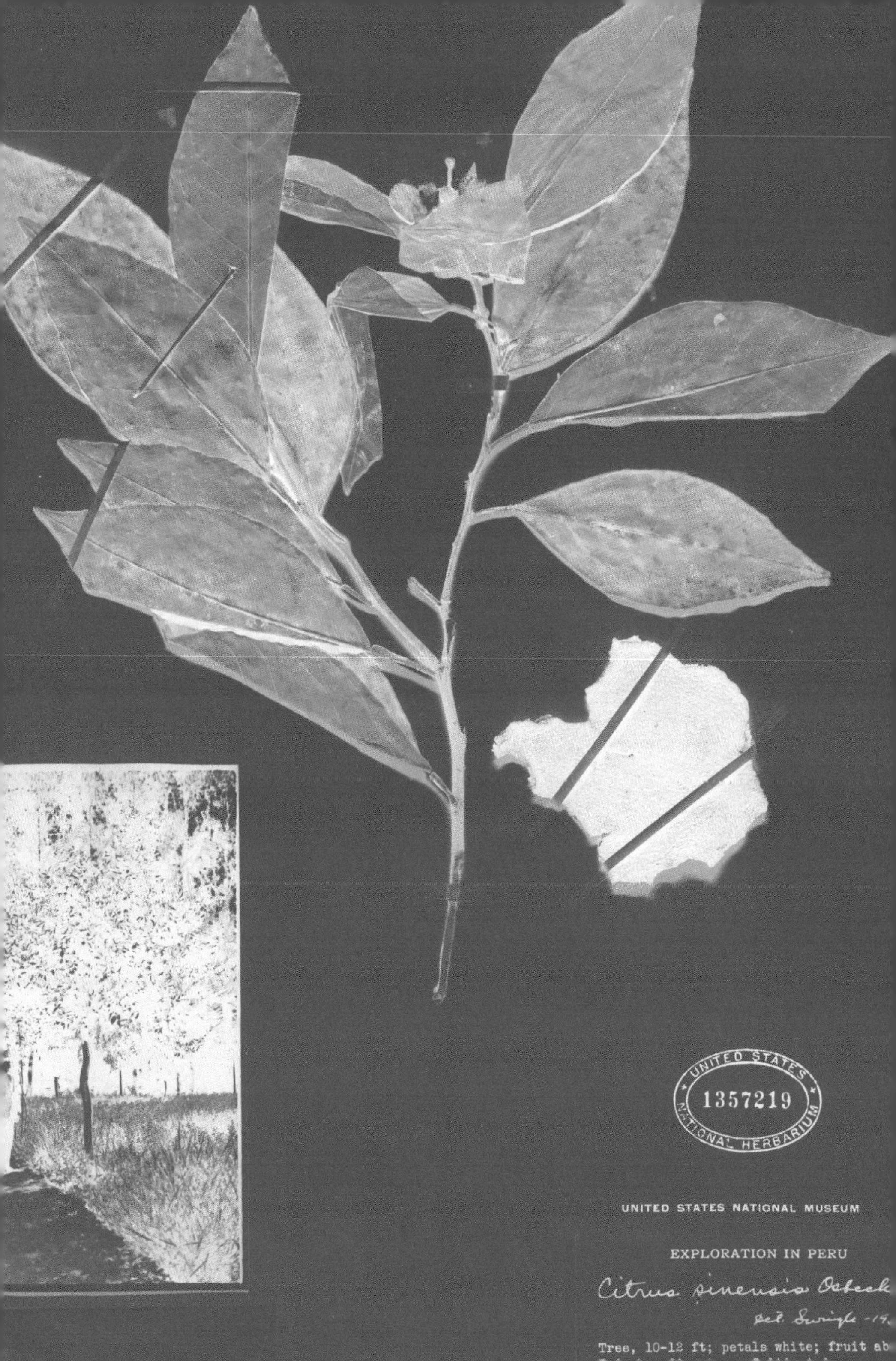

UNITED STATES
1357219
NATIONAL HERBARIUM
UNITED STATES NATIONAL MUSEUM
EXPLORATION IN PERU
Citrus sinensis Osbeck
det. Swingle -14,
Tree, 10-12 ft; petals white; fruit ab

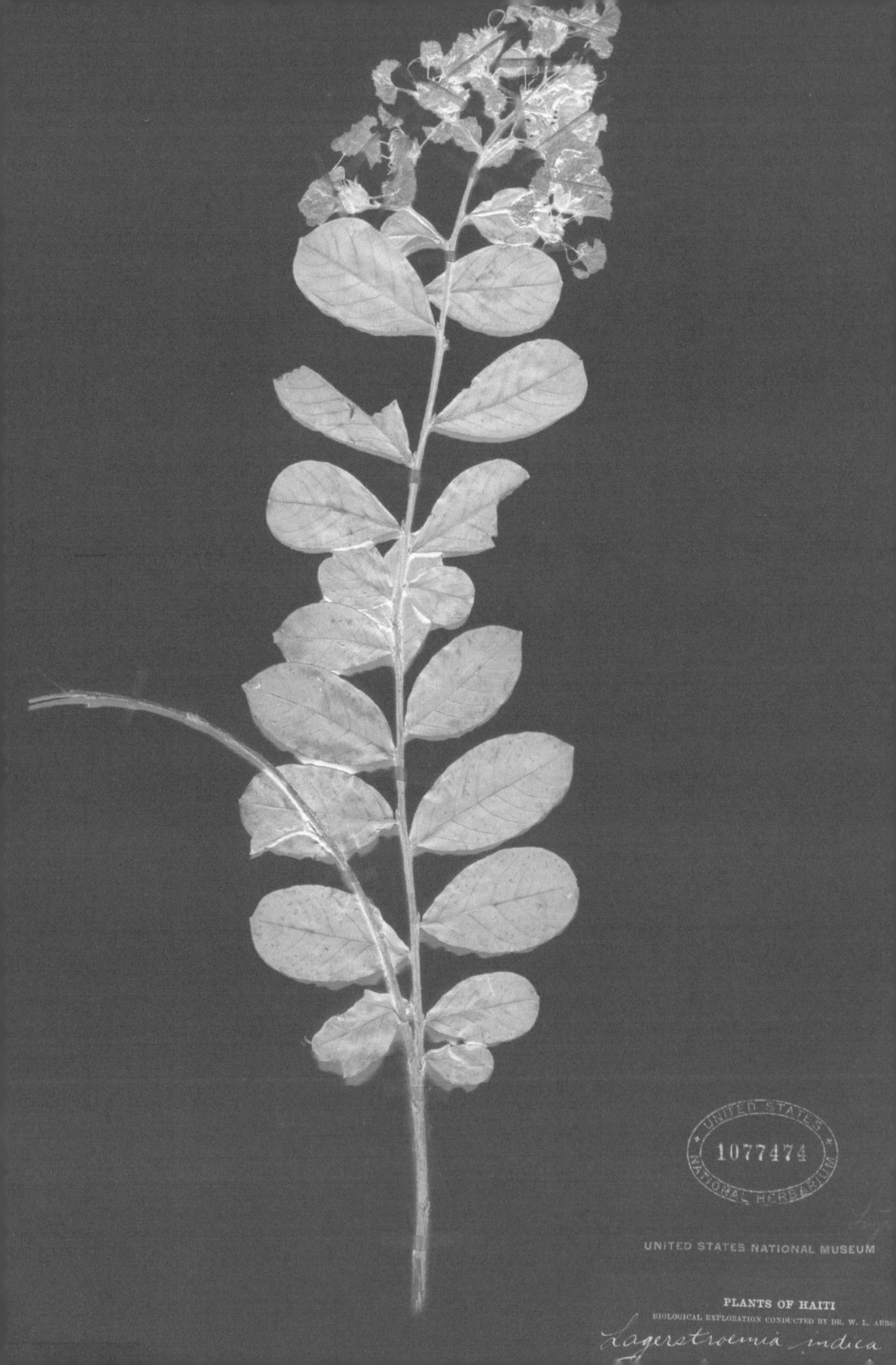

UNITED STATES NATIONAL MUSEUM

PLANTS OF HAITI

BIOLOGICAL EXPLORATION CONDUCTED BY DR. W. L. ABB

Lagerstroemia indica

II. Colonialism and Collecting

Returning to the words of Elspeth Haston, an herbarium specimen is a point in space and time. It is a beautiful thought and highlights what enlivens any form of archive, the notion that one can somehow return to something, bring it into the present, and preserve it for the future. One cannot consider the herbarium without thinking of a specific set of spaces and times, particularly the height of colonialism. Look up the largest herbariums, and you will see that the vast majority are located in Western Europe, and contain incredible amounts of material from Africa, Australasia, and the Americas. A recent paper by a diverse group of authors entitled "The colonial legacy of herbaria" describes the profound disparity between "where plant diversity naturally exists and where it is artificially housed and cataloged. This renders much of the world reliant on botanical knowledge and resources housed outside of their own borders." [1]

Some of the most avid collecting was done by botanists sent out on ships from European ports to find new territories and, thus, new resources. Botanical research, as one of the many activities pursued by colonizers, cannot be disentangled from the pursuit of capital - for cultural, scientific, and monetary gain. In many ways, the botanic gardens and herbariums of Europe, while being a driver of scientific study, were also one more spoke in the wheel of exploitation.

As European ships plied the oceans, laying claim to land that was not theirs, botanists gathered up plant life left and right, renaming it with no regard for those already there. Joseph Banks, an outspoken proponent of slavery, collected over 1,000 plant species when he sailed with Captain James Cook throughout the South Pacific in search of new territories for the British Empire to colonize. The HMS Bounty, famous for its mutiny, was purchased for a botanical mission, transporting breadfruit to the Caribbean as a cheap food source for enslaved people. In the second Anglo-Dutch war, the British held onto Manhattan while the Dutch kept the island of Pulau Run, an essential chain in their dominance over the spice trade. The bright, thorny bougainvillea, native to South America, discovered by the botanists Philibert Commerçon and Jeanne Baret (disguised as a man as women were not allowed on the expedition), bears a French name for the ship's admiral.

---

1. Park, Daniel & Feng, Xiao & Akiyama, Shinobu & Ardiyani, Marlina & Avendano, Neida & Barina, Zoltán & Bärtschi, Blandine & Belgrano, Manuel & Betancur, Julio & Bijmoer, Roxali & Bogaerts, Ann & Echeverría, Asunción & Danihelka, Jiří & Garg, Arti & Giblin, David & Gogoi, Rajib & Guggisberg, Alessia & Hyvarinen, Marko & James, Shelley & Davis, Charles. (2021). "The colonial legacy of herbaria." 10.1101/2021.10.27.466174.

In the cases of those Europeans who attempted even the slightest acknowledgment of Indigenous people's contributions, they were ignored, undercut, or ostracized. Joseph Hooker, the Director of the British botanic garden and research institute Kew Gardens, failed to listen to his colleague William Colenso's requests to use Maori terminology within the collection. His unwillingness to consider this led to misrepresentation and incorrect data throughout the collection. Wilhelm von Blandowski, an explorer and zoologist, pushed for the inclusion of Aboriginal classification and nomenclature in the work he sent off, citing the contributions of the Nyeri Nyeri people, only for it to be discarded.[2]

The collections of many institutions were first built during the late eighteenth into the nineteenth centuries. The digitization of herbaria around the world, a slow and expensive process, provides one possible corrective step to the original sin. In digitizing the information, many institutions are making their herbaria open and accessible to a much larger public, placing them in the commons. The question of who initiates and guides an herbarium is another step. The Karuk Tribal Herbaria, located at the Karuk People's Center Museum and their Department of Natural Resources is a recent project in partnership with the University of California Berkeley. The herbaria were founded to promote Indigenous sovereignty over cultural resources, land management, education, and plant revitalization in the Klamath River Basin. The plant specimens are organized by Yurok or Karuk name rather than plant family or genus.[3] Institutions are beginning to stage exhibitions with an emphasis on contextualizing their collections. Others are consulting communities and broadening the information they include. Some scholars are beginning to reevaluate naming conventions, pushing against the habit of first published names being favored over Indigenous ones or the frequency of actual colonizers being honored with scientific plant names.[4] Names are crucial to identification but also to history, place, and belonging. It will take a long time to refashion and rethink the methods and conventions at play but botany's history shows that change is natural and systems are never static.

---

2. von Zinnenburg Carroll, Khadija. "What Would Indigenous Taxonomy Look Like? The Case of Blandowski's Australia." Environment & Society Portal, Arcadia (2014), Rachel Carson Center for Environment and Society.

3. Mucioki, Megan. "Creating herbaria with tribes in the Klamath River Basin." Society for Ethnobotany (2019) https://ethnobiology.org/forage/blog/creating-herbaria-tribes-klamath-river-basin

4. Gillman, L.N., Wright, S.D. "Restoring indigenous names in taxonomy." Commun Biol 3,609 (2020). https://doi.org/10.1038/s42003-020-01344-y

schurb ohio
1960

schurb

x-14-60

Ley rp
on dryer
X-27-60

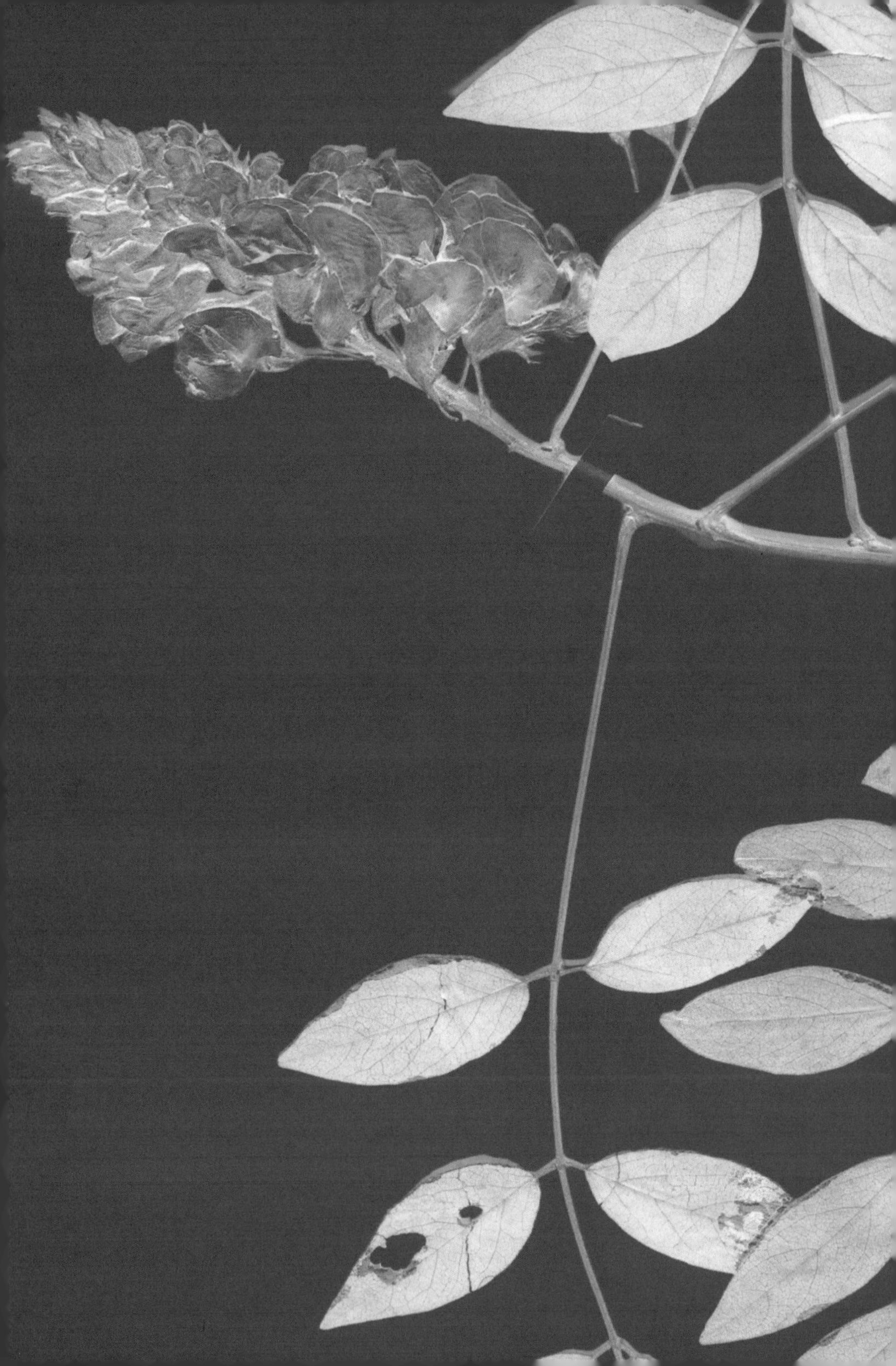

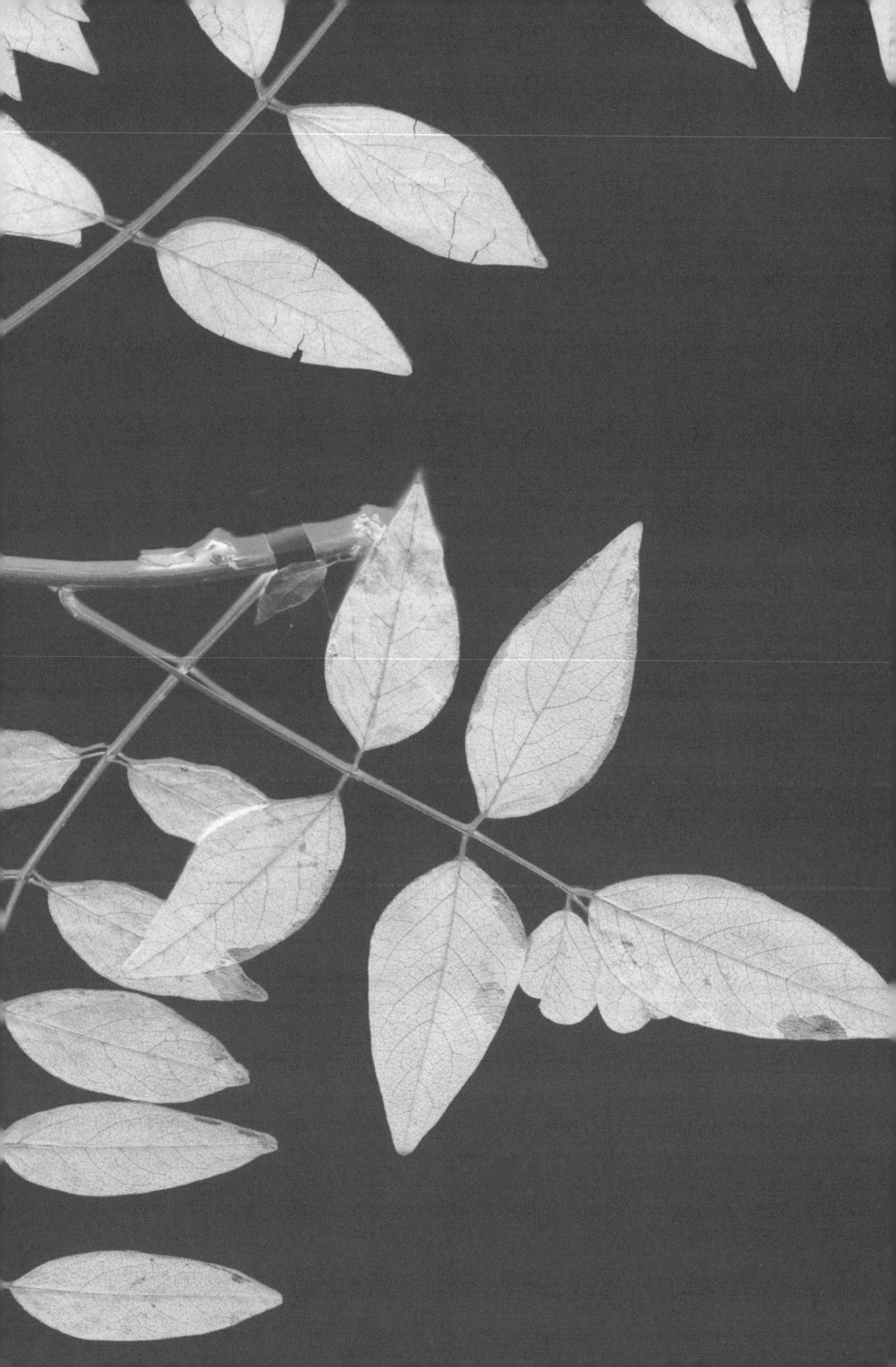

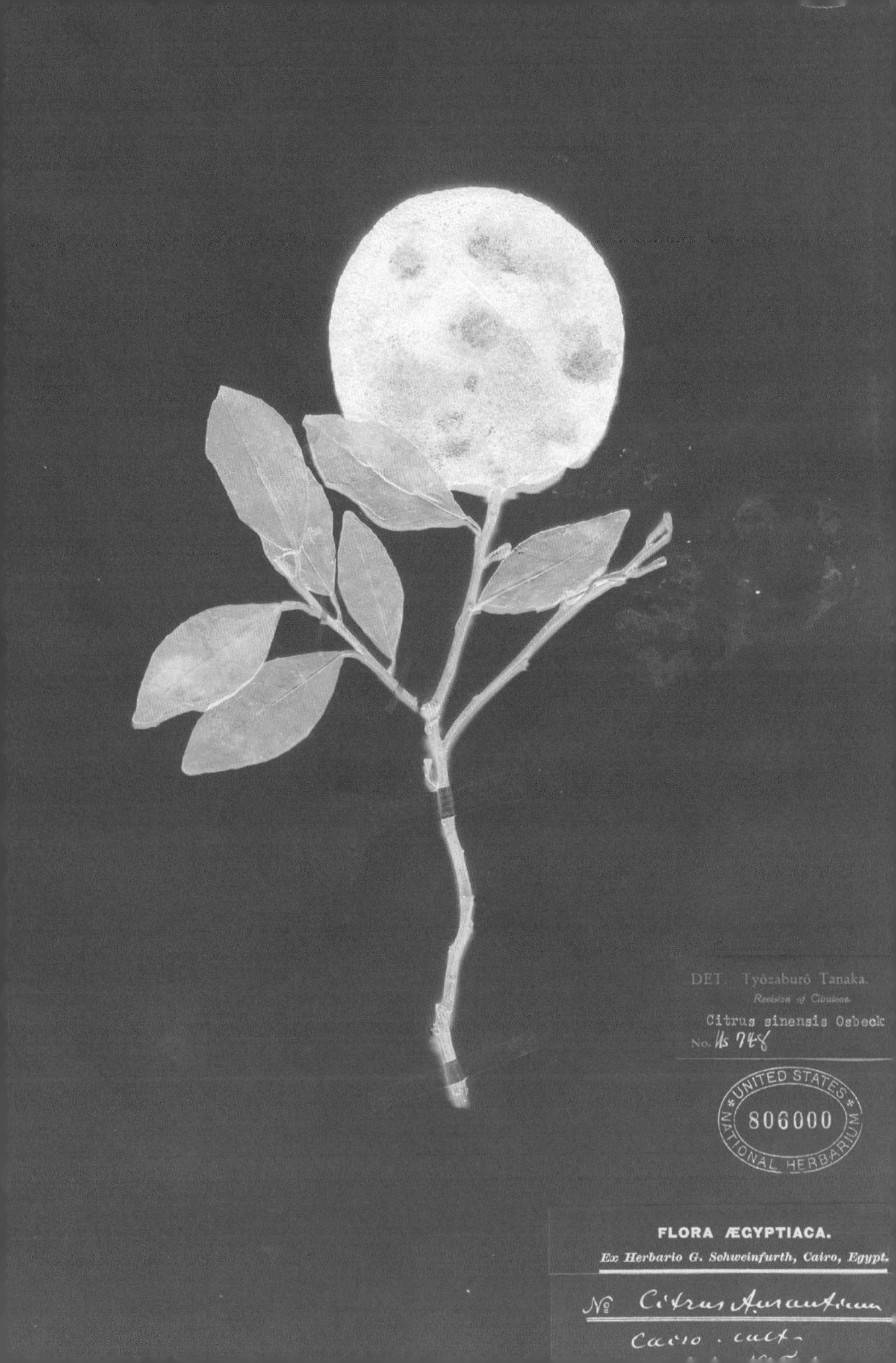

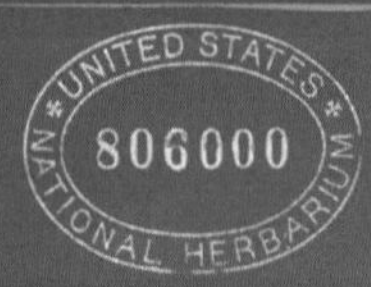
UNITED STATES
NATIONAL HERBARIUM
806000

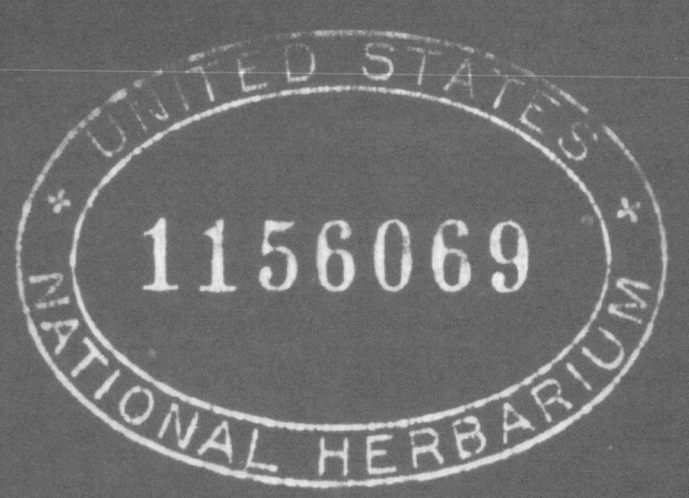

FLORA JAPONICA

...ia flori'bunda Mak...

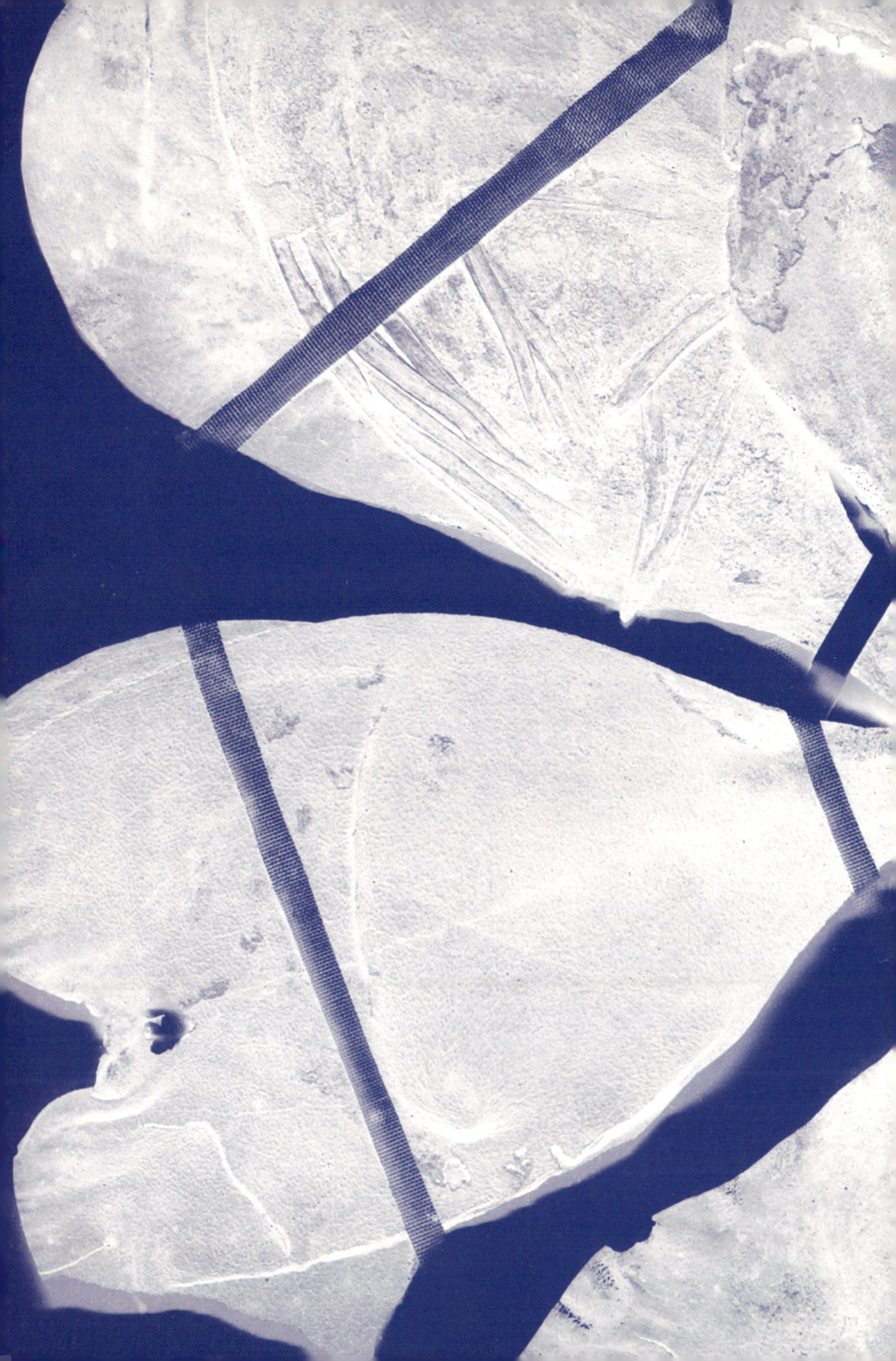

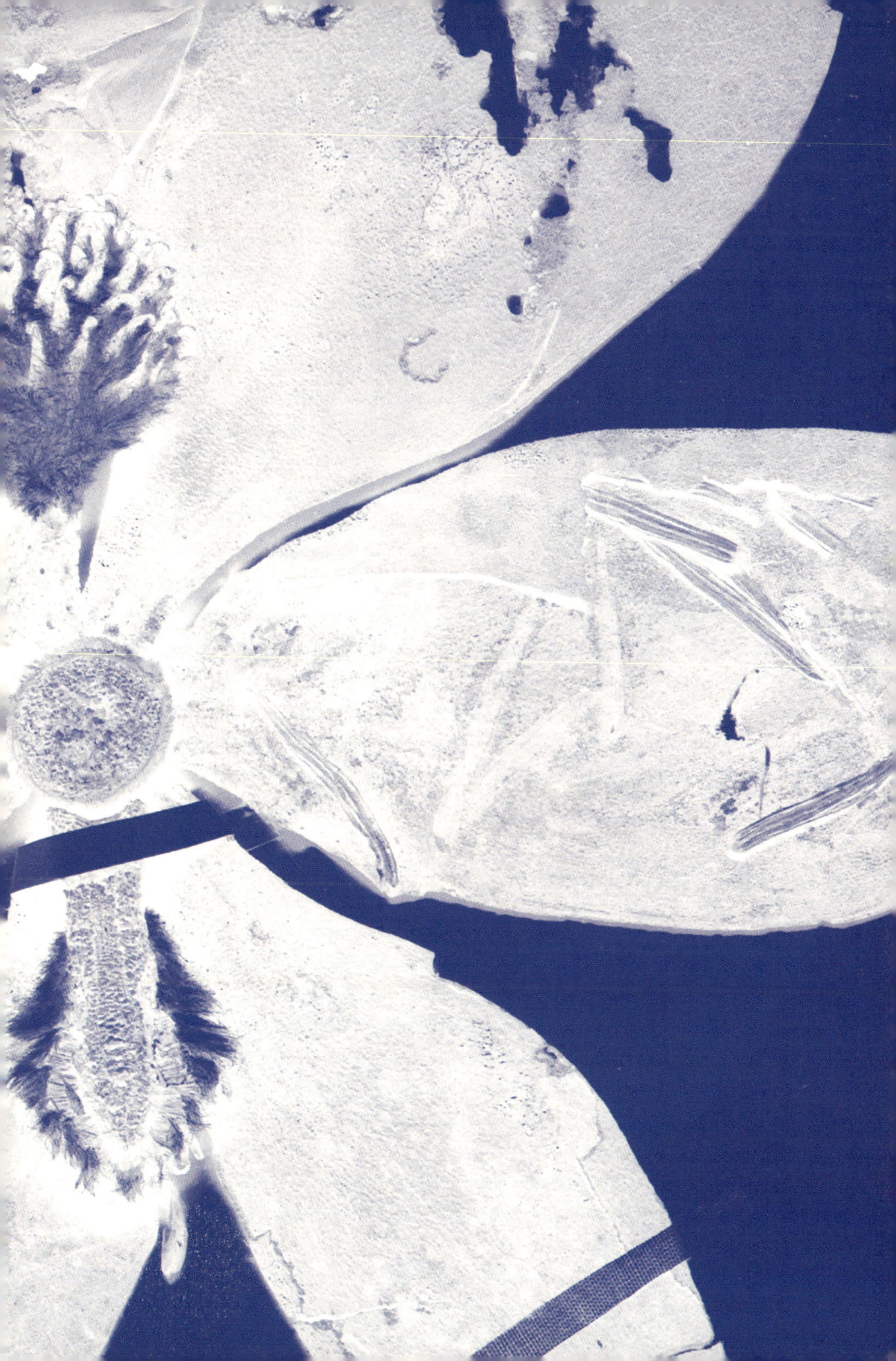

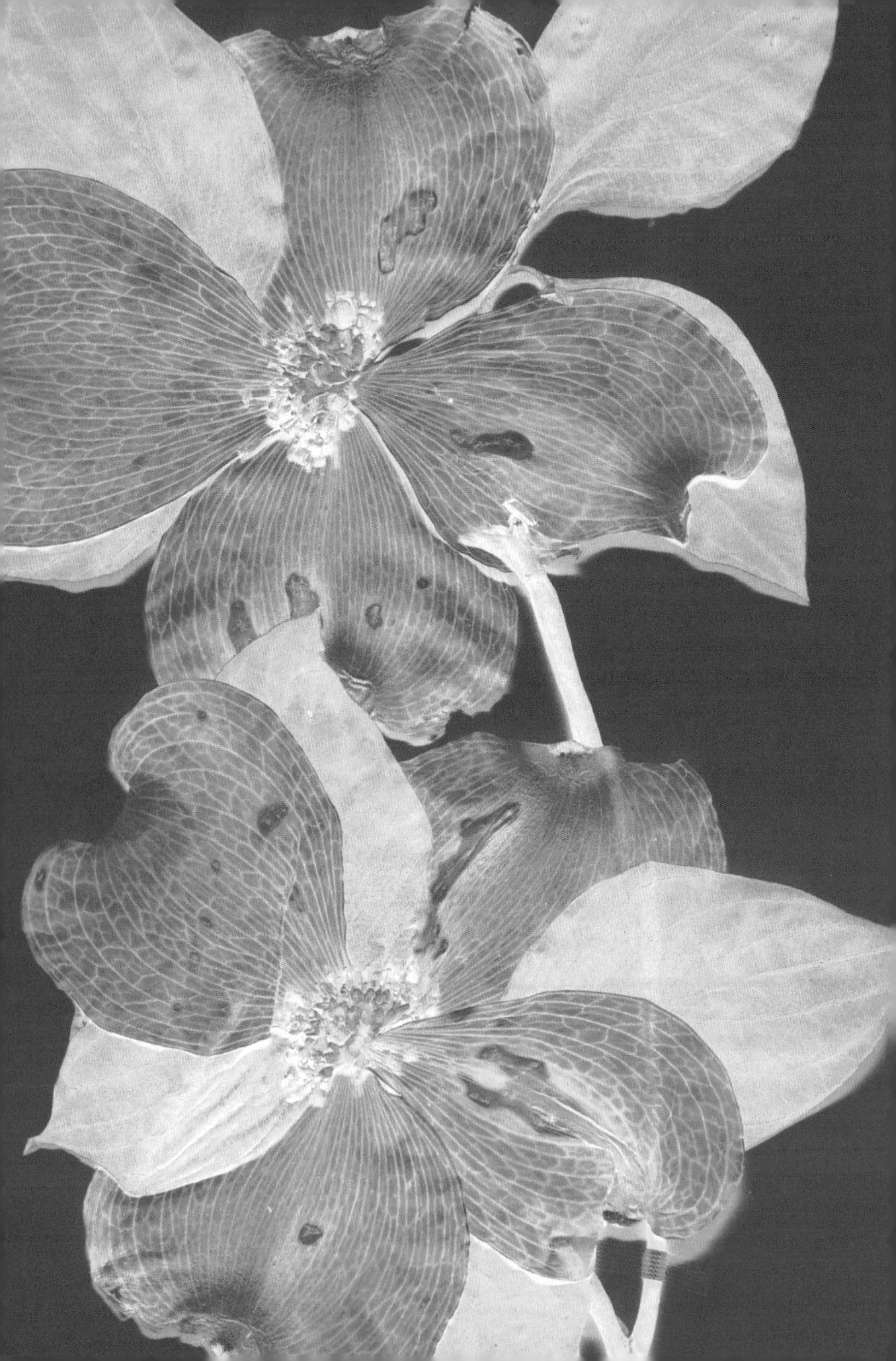

III. Repressed Botanists and Insult Comics

As a child, and sometimes still in my adult years, my name caused me a fair share of embarrassment and unnecessary stress. It seemed that English speakers could not wrap their heads around it. It was, as a not very good sales rep once told me, "too hard to remember." I came up with ways to rhyme it, accepted being called Mowgli, refused Maggie, and developed mnemonic devices through which I ended up being called Magazine for a full year of middle school gym classes. How hard could it be, as it was only one name? Imagine if these people had to remember eighteenth-century plant names.

Take the white pine, for example, a large conifer native to the Northeast. The Haudenosaunee called it the Tree of Peace as a symbol for the creation of the Five Nations Confederacy. In the early 1700s, Europeans referred to the white pine by a Latin name of *Pinus Americana quinis ex uno folliculo setis longis tenuibus triquetris as aunum angulum per totam* … it goes on. There was little to no standardization beyond the concept that a name should describe the plant; botanists seemed to be playing it by ear. The full Latin name of the white pine translated was "the American pine consisting of a single follicle of long, thin tricot bristles, each corner of which is roughened with very fine bristles along the entire length." Today we know the tree by the name Pinus strobus.

Scientists use a system of seven hierarchical levels to describe an organism: kingdom, phylum, class, order, family, genus, and species. Seven is less than the Latin paragraph above, but is still a bit unwieldy. This is where Carl Linnaeus came in. Linnaeus, a Swedish botanist, is considered the father of taxonomy, the science of naming, describing, and classifying. He came up with a new system of classification and one of naming. In *Systema Naturae*, first published in 1735, Linnaeus proposed a system of classification based on plants' reproductive organs, counting their pistils and stamens (the system has been replaced with something far more scientific, but it was a decent start). Prior to this, plants were classified based on appearance, use, or whether or not they were edible. Linnaeus decided upon an empirical method of identification that would simplify classification and allow ever more people to learn how to identify plants. With basic familiarity, one could identify plants with his system. And yet there was a tremendous amount of pushback against it. Many botanists revealed themselves as prudes, calling Linnaeus lewd and his observations "too smutty."

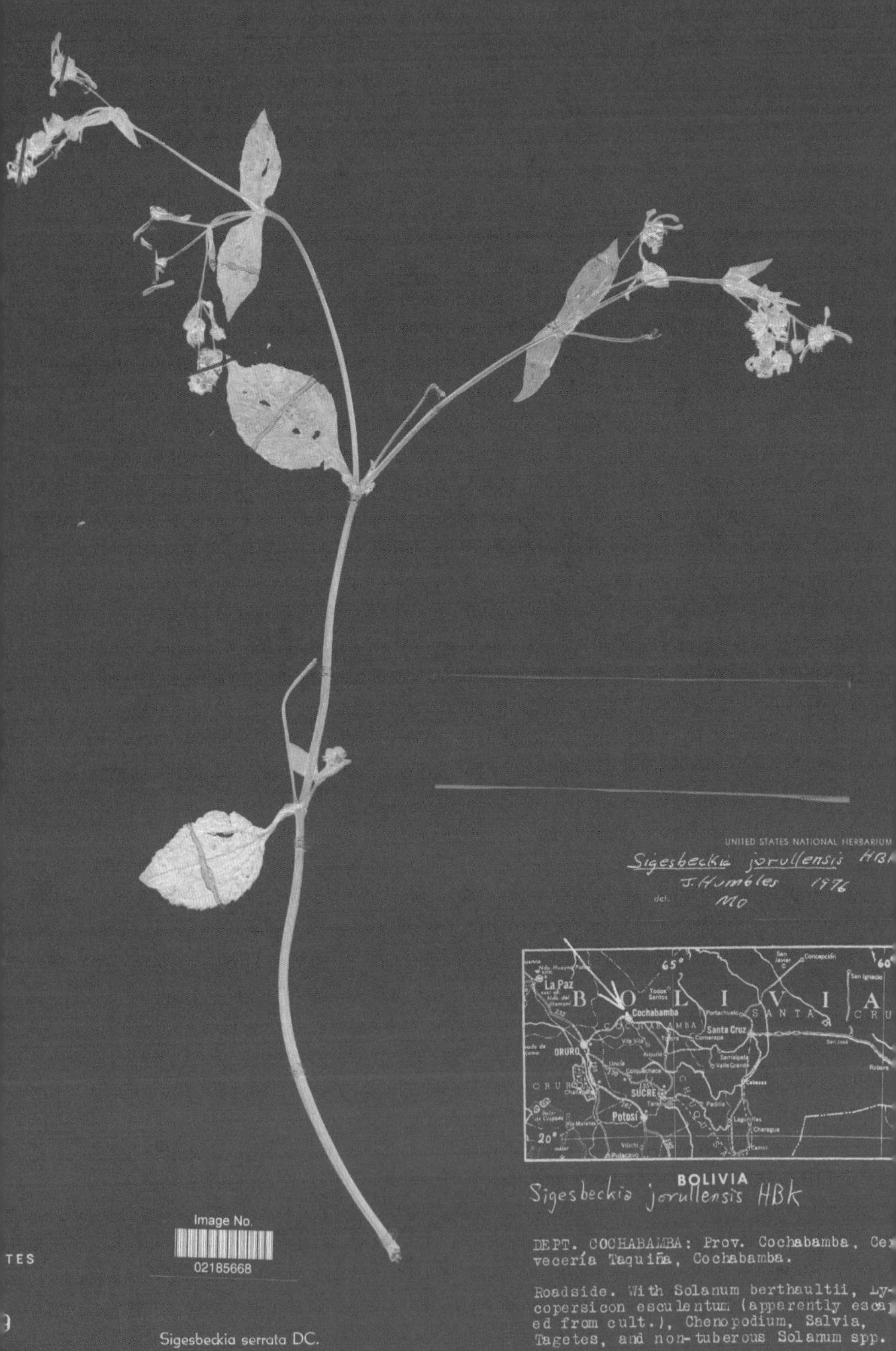

UNITED STATES NATIONAL HERBARIUM
Sigesbeckia jorullensis HBK
J. Humbles 1976
det. MO
BOLIVIA
Sigesbeckia jorullensis HBK
DEPT. COCHABAMBA: Prov. Cochabamba, Cer-
vecería Taquiña, Cochabamba.
Roadside. With Solanum berthaultii, Ly-
copersicon esculentum (apparently escap-
ed from cult.), Chenopodium, Salvia,
Tagetes, and non-tuberous Solanum spp.
Sigesbeckia serrata DC.
Image No.
02185668
TES

One of the most scandalized was the German botanist Johann Georg Sieges-beck who called the system "loathsome harlotry."[1]

Linnaeus broke up plants into kingdoms and then classes and moved away from the concept that a name should provide a detailed description of every plant. He used a binomial structure, a two-word name, wherein the first name refers to the genus or generic name and the second to the species name. He often honored other botanists and scientists with his naming structure. *Rudbeckia*, or coneflower or black-eyed Susan, was named after Linnaeus' patron and fellow botanist Olof Rudbeck the Younger. He described the naming as such, "I have chosen a noble plant in order to recall your merits and the services you have ren-dered, a tall one to give an idea of your stature, and I wanted it to be one which branched and which flowered and fruited freely, to show that you cultivated not only the sciences but also the humanities. Its rayed flowers will bear witness that you shone among savants like the sun among the stars; its perennial roots will remind us that each year sees you live again through new works."[2]

He was not the only botanist to name a plant as a tribute. The French botanist Charles Plumier was the first Westerner to name the tree that we now know as a Magnolia. On the island of Martinique, Plumier christened the tree, *Magnolia amplimissimo flore albo, fructo caeruleo* (the magnolia with large white flowers and blue fruit - today known as the *Magnolia dodecapetala*). He was working before Lin-naeus' binomial breakthrough and named the tree after the French Huguenot botanist Pierre Magnol who was one of the first to come up with the concept of plant families. Linnaeus kept the tribute in his simplification, and the genus is still known as Magnolia; the species breaks down to *grandiflora*, *dodecapetala*, *liliiflora*, *coco*, and *figo*, amongst others.

As much as one could honor with a name, Linnaeus could also insult, and so he returned to Siegesbeck, whose morals were so greatly offended by the sexual classification system. Linnaeus, in an act of retaliation, named a pesky, sticky weed *Siegesbeckia* as payback for the German botanist's criticism. The feud esca-lated after he mistakenly sent Siegesbeck a packet of seeds which he had labeled *Cuculus ingratus* (ungrateful cuckoo).

---

1. Heard, Stephen B. *Charles Darwin's Barnacle and David Bowie's Spider: How Scientific Names Celebrate Adventurers, Heroes, and Even a Few Scoundrels*. Yale University Press, 2020

2. Blunt, Wilfrid. *The Compleat Naturalist: A Life of Linnaeus*, Viking Press, 1971

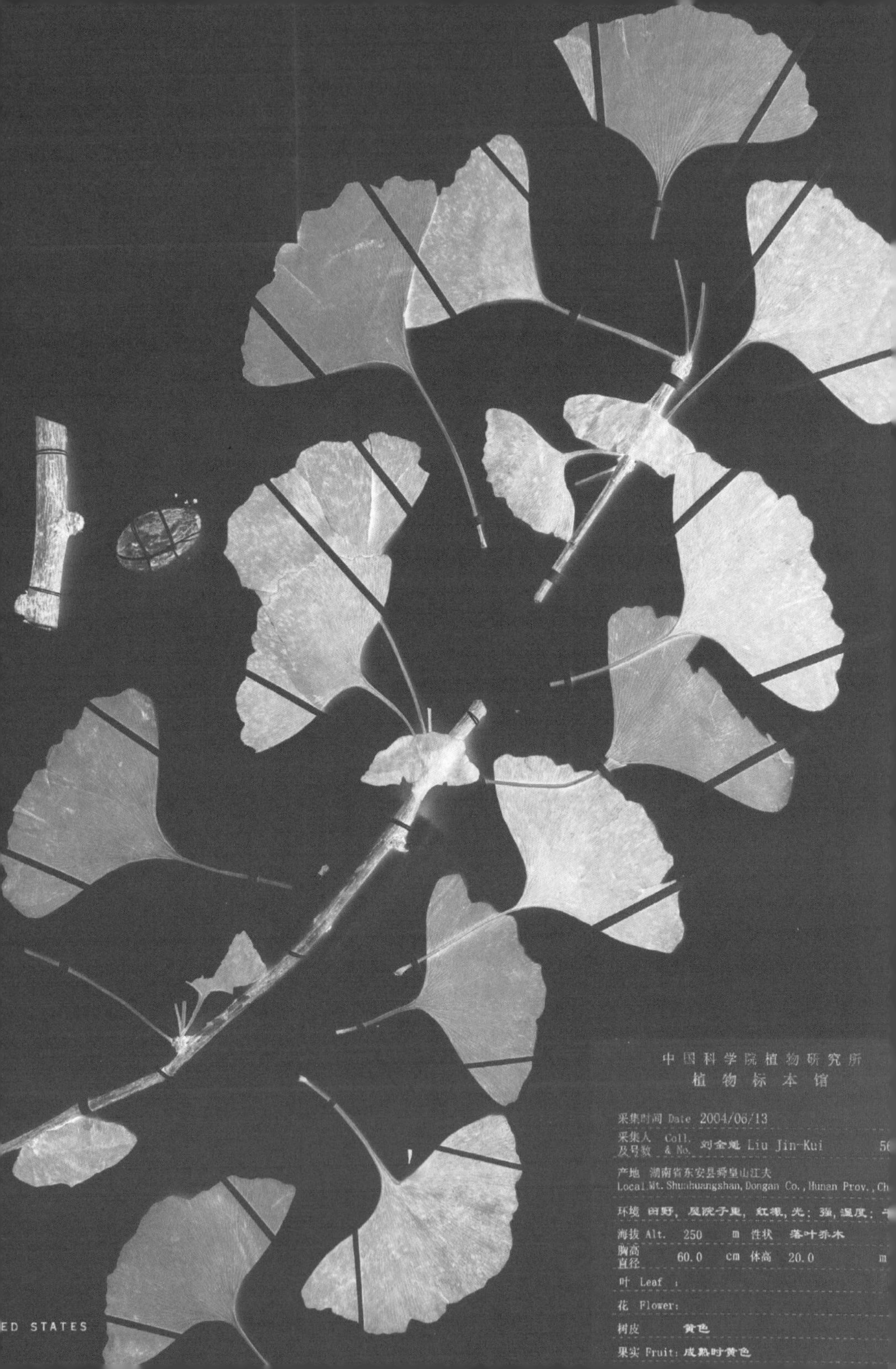
ED STATES
中国科学院植物研究所
植物标本馆
采集时间 Date 2004/06/13
采集人 Coll. 刘金魁 Liu Jin-Kui 56
及号数 & No.
产地 湖南省东安县舜皇山江夫
Local.Mt. Shunhuangshan, Dongan Co., Hunan Prov., Ch
环境 田野，层院子里，红壤，光：强，温度：
海拔 Alt. 250 m 性状 落叶乔木
胸高
直径 60.0 cm 体高 20.0 m
叶 Leaf :
花 Flower:
树皮 黄色
果实 Fruit: 成熟时黄色

Upon their growth the seeds revealed themselves to be none other than the weed *Siegesbeckia*.[3]

Siegesbeck was not the only one targeted. Stephen Heard writes about a handful of botanists who were already dead when Linnaeus came for them. Francisco Hernandez's "unproductive work" inspired *Hernandia*, a tree of large, lush leaves but somewhat hidden flowers. *Dorstenia*, a relative of the mulberry, was named for Theodor Dorsten, "whose flowers are not showy, as though they were faded and past their prime which recalls the work of Dorsten." For Linnaeus, relieving scientific names of the weight of description was important but they still managed to slip in here and there.

Linnaeus wasn't alone in deploying this form of spite naming. Wilhelm von Blandowski, whose attempts to include Aboriginal naming of species caused issues (as did his apparent lack of general social skills), chose to name fish samples that were described as "slimy, slippery and easily recognized by their low forehead, big belly and sharp spine," after members of the Philosophical Institute of Victoria. The institute's council censured him but were unable to find the votes to expel him.

Through all of this, it's not hard to see that the vast majority of plants are named for white, Western men. As time goes on, there have been natural correctives, more women have entered the sciences for one, but the disparity is still vast. There are species and plants named for Indigenous peoples as a plural more than individuals; when individuals are cited, they are almost always kings, queens, or leaders. But to assume that a "Western" notion of naming is a one size fits all solution is not the answer. In some cultures, the concept of naming a plant for a single person is offensive; in others, a waiting time must be observed before using a name as a tribute. Being more fully aware of where names and conventions come from and how to consult others is one step forward. As the journey to binomial nomenclature shows, a path is never simply a straight line, especially when drawn by humans with their virtues and sins.

---

3. Wulf, Andrea. *The Brothers Gardeners: A Generation of Gentlemen Naturalists and the Birth of an Obsession*. Knopf Doubleday Publishing Group, 2010

4. Heard, Stephen B. *Charles Darwin's Barnacle and David Bowie's Spider: How Scientific Names Celebrate Adventurers, Heroes, and Even a Few Scoundrels*. Yale University Press, 2020

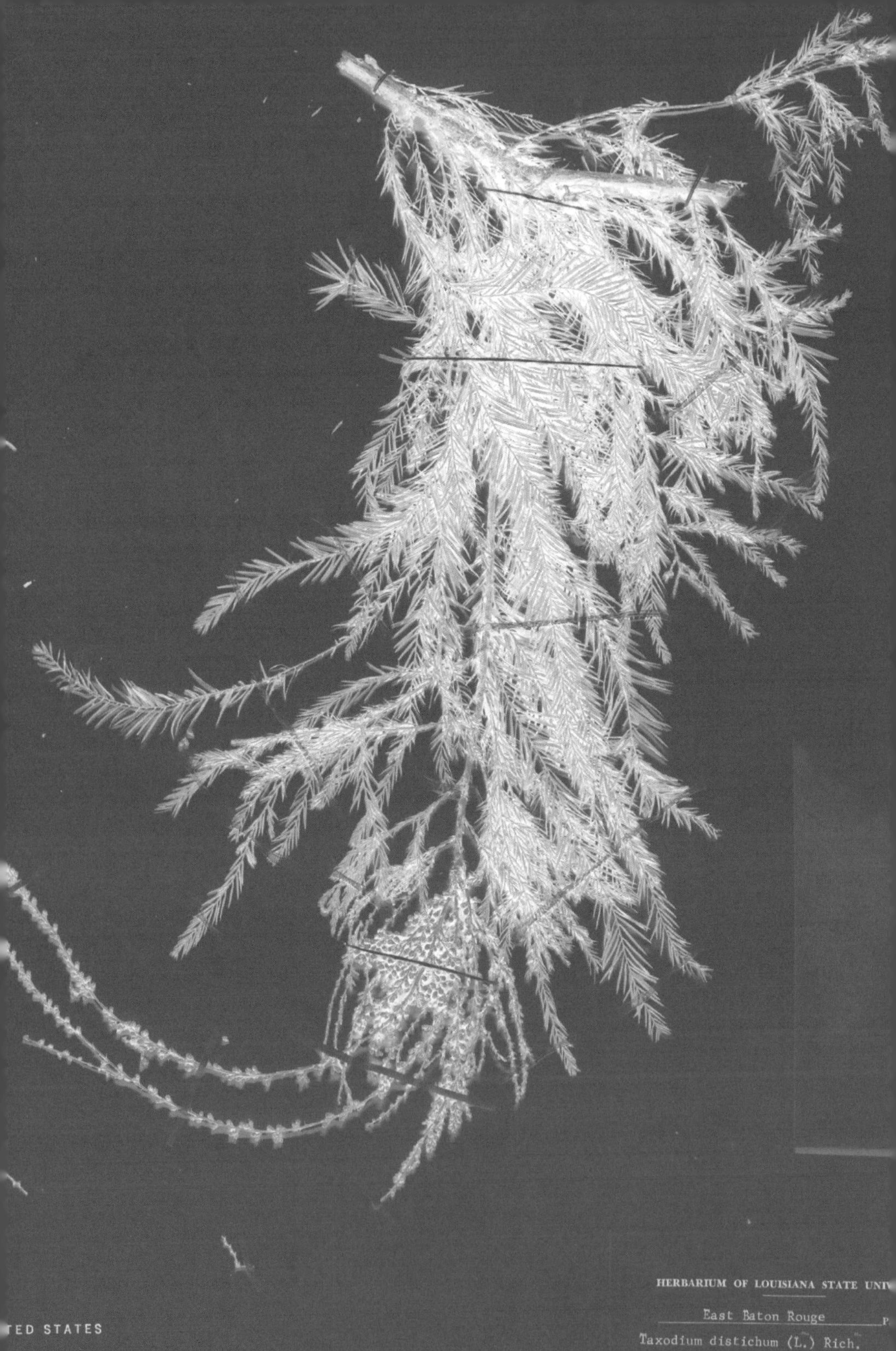
HERBARIUM OF LOUISIANA STATE UNIV
East Baton Rouge
Taxodium distichum (L.) Rich.
TED STATES

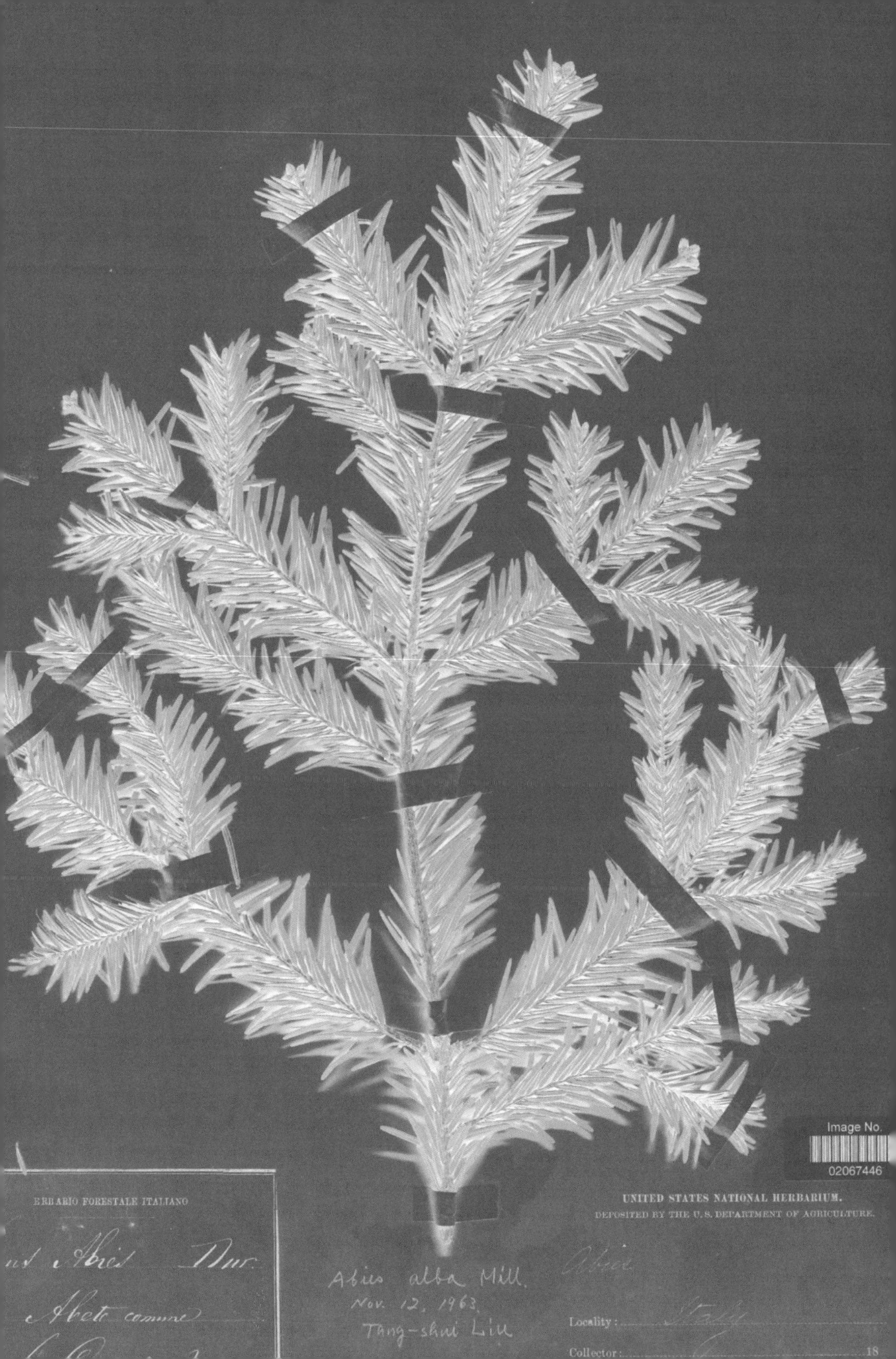
ERBARIO FORESTALE ITALIANO
UNITED STATES NATIONAL HERBARIUM.
DEPOSITED BY THE U. S. DEPARTMENT OF AGRICULTURE.
Abies alba Mill.
Nov. 12, 1963.
Tang-shui Liu
Locality :
Collector :
Image No.
02067446

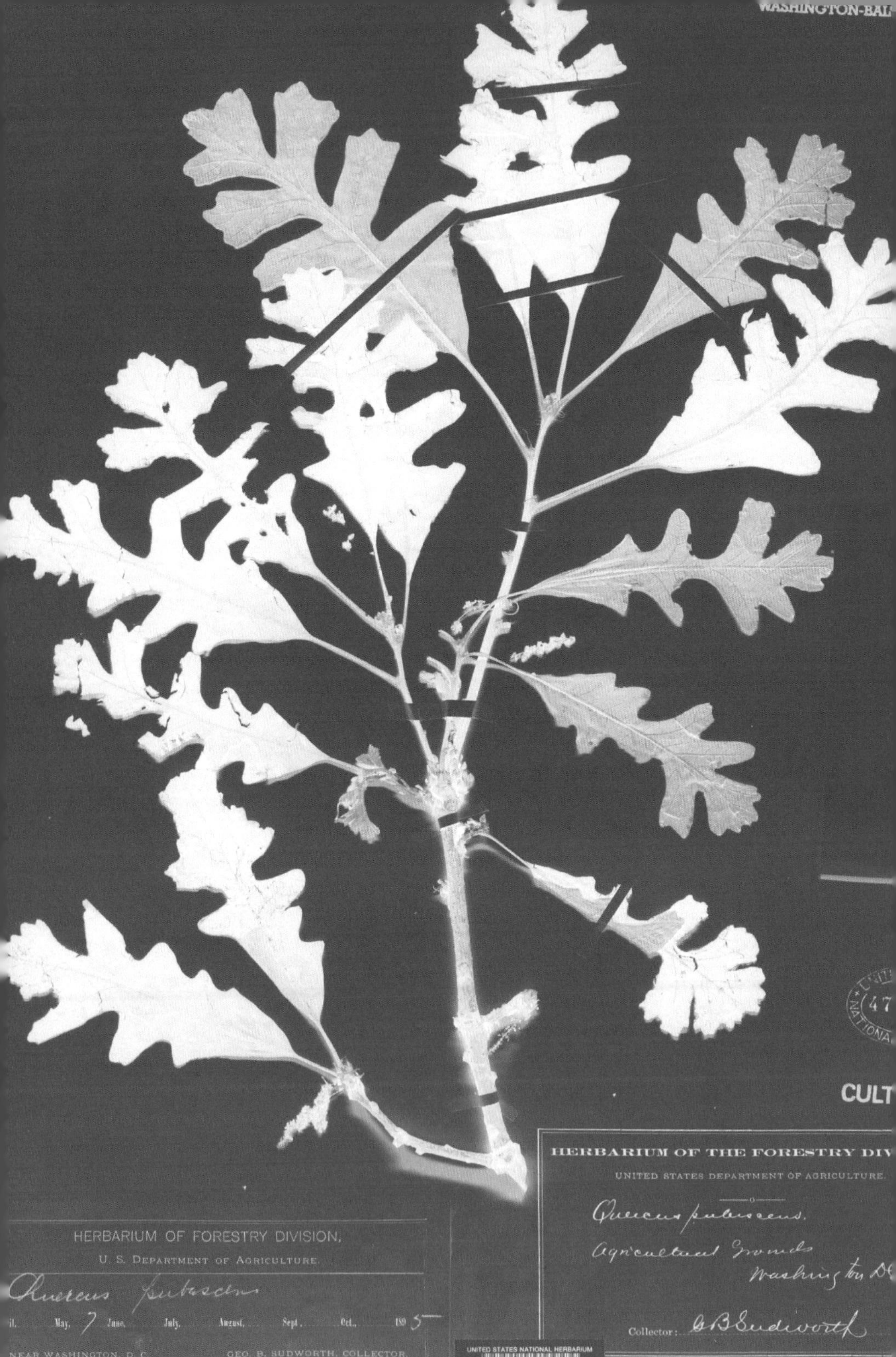

WASHINGTON-BAL
CULT
HERBARIUM OF THE FORESTRY DIV
UNITED STATES DEPARTMENT OF AGRICULTURE.
Quercus pubescens.
Agricultural Grounds
Washington DC
Collector: G. B. Sudworth
HERBARIUM OF FORESTRY DIVISION,
U. S. DEPARTMENT OF AGRICULTURE.
Quercus pubescens
May, June, July, August, Sept., Oct., 189 5
NEAR WASHINGTON, D. C.   GEO. B. SUDWORTH, COLLECTOR.
UNITED STATES NATIONAL HERBARIUM

Citrus decumana

Chadec

cultivated New Or...

A. B. LANGLOIS,
Pointe a la Hache P. O., La.

CULTIVATED

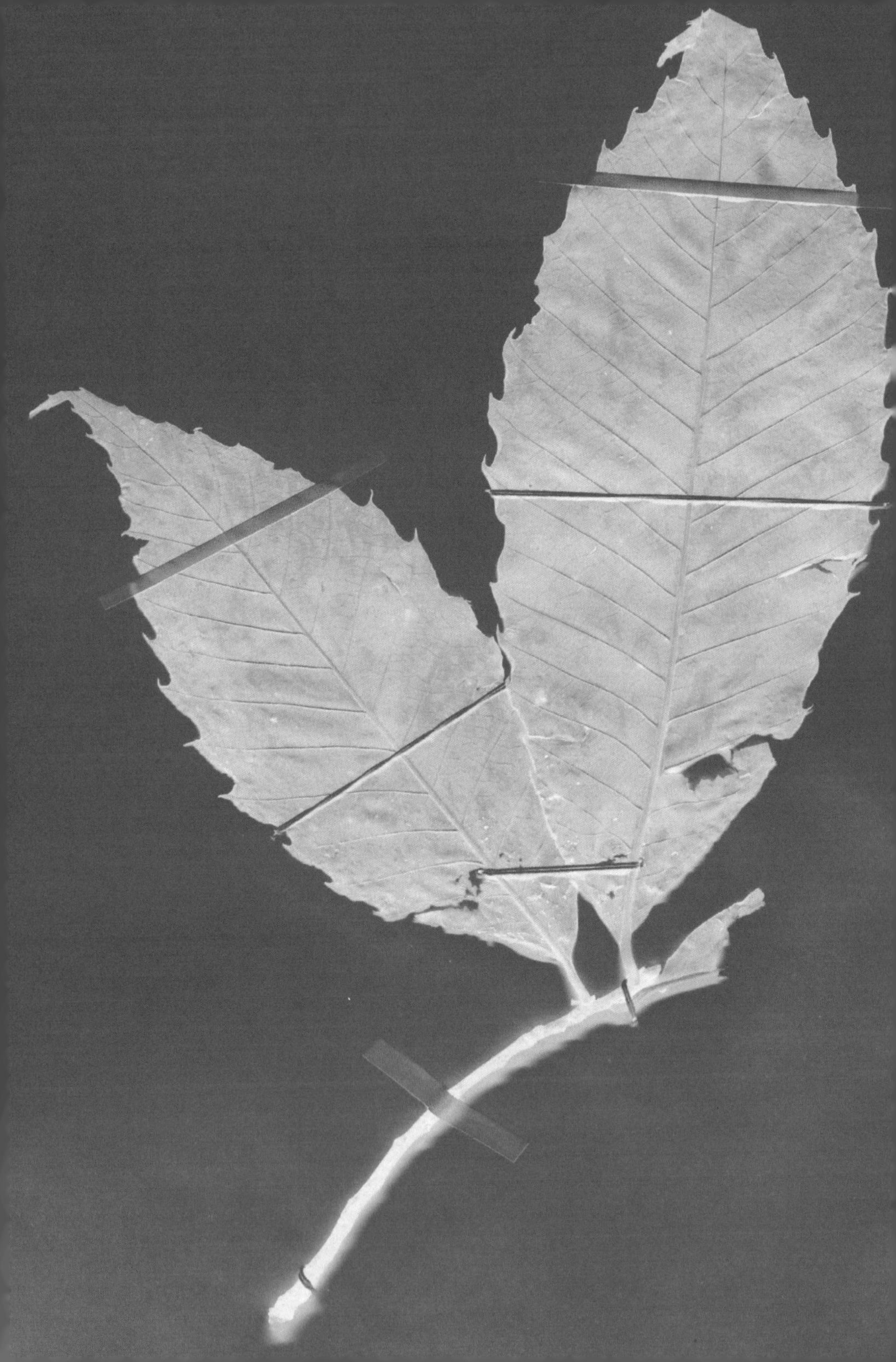

HERBERT F. DARLING
GENERAL CONTRACTOR
131 California Drive
Williamsville, N. Y.

October 19, 1959

United States Department of Agriculture
Forest Service
Albert G. Snow, Jr.
Research Center Leader
RFD 2 Box 263
Laurel, Maryland

Attention: Mr. J. D. Diller

Dear Sir:

Thank you for your letter of 3 September, 1959.

I am sending herewith leaves and burrs from the 8" chestnut. Please tell me if it is surely American. Just lately this tree shows some blight on trunk. Can small individual spots such as this be treated to kill it?

I will be very happy to send scions in February. - Just give me instructions.

Each of two other young trees- 2" show blight where wounded by falling branches.

Very truly yours,

Herbert F. Darling. HR

Encl.
HFD/lh

IV. Very Truly Yours : The Herbarium in Use

I am sending herewith leaves and burrs, wrote Herbert Darling on October 19, 1959. *I have enclosed a picture and a story that ran in the local paper*, wrote Jane Sutton on September 26, 1960. Both asked the US Department of Agriculture's Forest Service about American chestnut trees. Both are examples of herbaria in everyday use. But let's start at the beginning. The American Chestnut Blight is considered one of the greatest ecological catastrophes in US history, causing the death of over three billion trees. In the early 1900s, imported chestnut trees brought a parasitic fungus that fell their American cousins in huge numbers. Pre-blight, one in every four trees in the East was a chestnut. The trees proliferated and towered over others in forests. The wood was rot-resistant, straight-grained, and used for everything from railroad ties and telephone poles to housing, furniture and coffins. The nuts the tree produced fed animals, insects, and birds and powered local industries. The blight strangled the trees' vasculature, crippling their ability to circulate nutrients and water. The devastation changed local economies and reshaped the landscape. "With the death of the chestnut," the historian Donald Davis wrote in 2005, "an entire world did die, eliminating subsistence practices that had been viable in the Appalachian Mountains for more than four centuries."[1] The tree is considered functionally extinct in the sense that though the blight does not affect the root system, allowing small saplings to sprout, it has effectively killed the ability of the tree to reach sizes beyond shrub stature.
By the middle of the last century, a call was put out for citizens to contact the Forest Service if they knew of American chestnut trees still producing nuts. Letters, leaves, and burrs began to appear. The specimens and their corresponding letters were observed, pressed, and placed on boards to join the herbarium. Scientists, sent to investigate, discovered blight, or where the trees were producing nuts, they turned out to be hybrids. The quest to bring back the American chestnut continues. Genetic engineering, crossbreeding, crop rotations, and more have been researched for decades. For every success, an attendant failure seems to appear, but progress is being made, however slowly. The herbarium acts as a history book moving from healthy specimens of the 1800s to queries on sickly trees as the 20th century progressed.

Herbaria were once called *hortus mortus*, a dead garden, but these specific pages show the desire to save the garden from death. The herbarium is a collection of plants but also people. It features their handwriting and interests, their cares and concerns. An archive once called a dead garden is alive if you look closely enough.

---

1. Popkin, Gabriel. "Can Genetic Engineering Bring Back the American Chestnut?" New York Times Magazine. April 30, 2020

Sept. 26, 1960

Dear Mr. Diller,

Enclosed you will find a Branch and Bur to be identified I have enclosed a picture and a story that ran in the local paper to help you with identification.

thank you,
Jane E Sutton
Shavertown R.
Boothwyn 10
Penna.

will find

to be id

a picture

in the loca

ith identifi

thank y

Telephone: 521 Sta.-Sta.
Watkins Glen N Y 196

Estab. 1916

Van Dyne
nserv.Albany
    (Spence Duncan)
Knapp,PRR,Sodus Pt

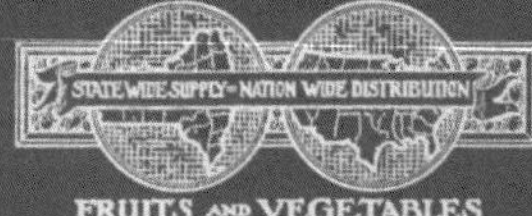

J. S. NEILL CO.

UNIFORM QUALITY

STATE WIDE SUPPLY — NATION WIDE DISTRIBUTION

FRUITS AND VEGETABLES

WATKINS GLEN, NEW YORK   Oct. 1, 1960

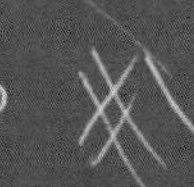

Mr. J.D.Diller, Pathologist
U.S.Dept of Agriculture,
Forest Service
NORTHEASTERN FOREST EXPERIMENT STA
RFD 2, Box 283
Laurel, Md.

Dear Sir,-

        At long last, I enclosed 2/3 pressed

leaves from the Chestnut Tree at Sodus Point, -

William Knapp, c/o PRR that place, brought them

here.   I have also branches so you could ex-

amine wood if you wanted to.

        The leaves marked No.1 have card at-
tached reading
                "OLD NATIVE CHESTNUT TREE, only
                living one in country known to
                white man, or otherwise".

        This #1 sample is from tree by PRR
sta. Sodus Point, about 30'. Mr. Knapp got nuts
from it last year. He is going to get nuts this
Fall and send to me.

        I also enclose samples from Chinese
Chestnut Tree marked #2, also on a naber's place
at Sodus Point.

        I wish you would do something about
preserving this tree.   The NY State Conservation
Dept. was inquiring about Chestnut Trees sometime
since and I believe I wrote them but heard nothing.
They have other fish to fry apparently"   But,
Ed Van Dyne of Troy,Pa. sez you are "Mr.Chestnut"
himself, and I leave it in your hands.
                Sincerely,
                    J.S.NEILL CO.

If you dont want the nuts hes going to send me, I'm
going plant 'em myself. I should live so long to see the fruit

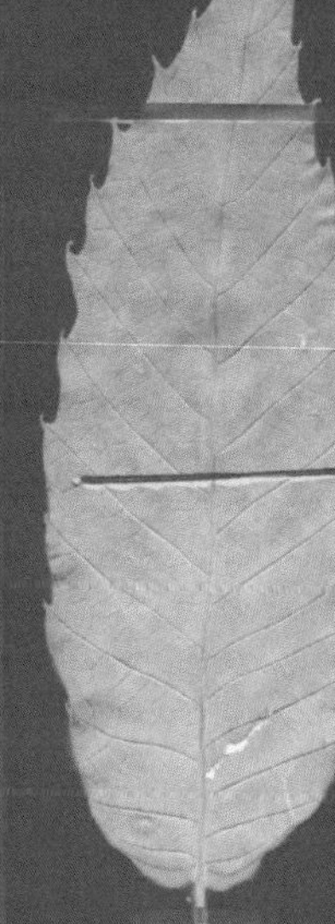

Quercus pubescens, Downy oak

Ginkgo biloba

Lagerstromea indica, Crape myrtle

Sigesbeckia serrata, St. Pauls wort

Wisteria floribunda

Taxodium distichum, Bald cypress

Albus balsamea, Balsam fir

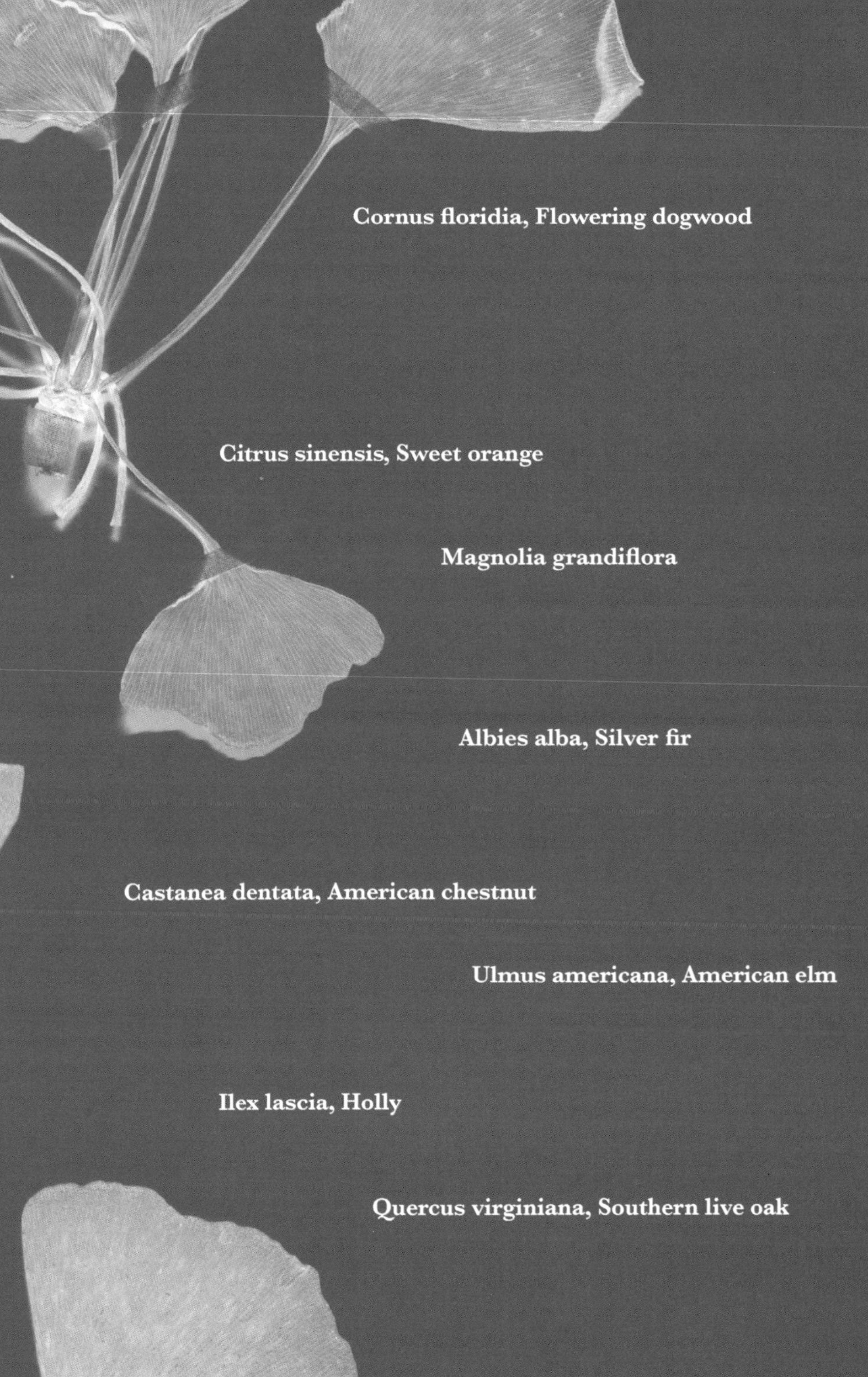

Cornus floridia, Flowering dogwood
Citrus sinensis, Sweet orange
Magnolia grandiflora
Albies alba, Silver fir
Castanea dentata, American chestnut
Ulmus americana, American elm
Ilex lascia, Holly
Quercus virginiana, Southern live oak

V. How to Herbarium

To make an herbarium is to create a record, an archive. It can be a collection based around beauty, a tribute to elevate what others might call weeds. It can keep track of adventures or changes in the area. It may remind one of what a space was like at a point in time. It can be a source of inspiration, an exercise, and a lesson in creativity.

It can be a means of connecting and understanding where we live.

Instructions

1. Get ready to collect plants.
      - Don't collect in wet weather as plants will be harder to dry.
      - Don't collect endangered plants or those in protected status !

2. Take a photograph of where you collected the plant.

3. Note down essential details about the plant and its habitat.
      - What color is it and is it grouped with others?
      - How tall is the plant?
      - What is around it?

4. Take a cutting.

5. Prepare the plant for pressing.
      - Clean the cutting to remove any dirt or insects.
      - Dry the plant by patting it down to sop up liquid.

6. Prepare a plant press.
      - This can be an actual press with wooden boards or
       even a set of heavy books (give those dictionaries a task).
      - Place a flat piece of cardboard on top of a wooden board
       and 2 sheets of newspaper, tissue, or blotting paper down.
      - Place your plant on top, and then place two more sheets of
       newspaper, tissue, or blotting paper on top.
      - Place your second board or heavy book on top of that
       and then place more heavy books or bricks on top.

---

1. Harvard's Houghton Library is home to the poet Emily Dickinson's herbarium completed when she was just 14 years old. A digital facsimile is viewable online. https://iiif.lib.harvard.edu/manifests/view/drs:4184689$9i

7. Wait anywhere between 2 days to 3 weeks for the plants to fully dry out.
- You can check on the plants every day or two and swap out the
newspaper if needed.
- You must remove all moisture to avoid rot.

8. When ready to mount the plant onto paper, brush the plants with
a non-acidic adhesive and press them onto a sheet of acid-free paper.
- You can also use linen tape to secure sections of the plant.

9. Create a card to transcribe the information you collected.
- Include the plant's name, height, width, color,
date, and the location of where you collected it.

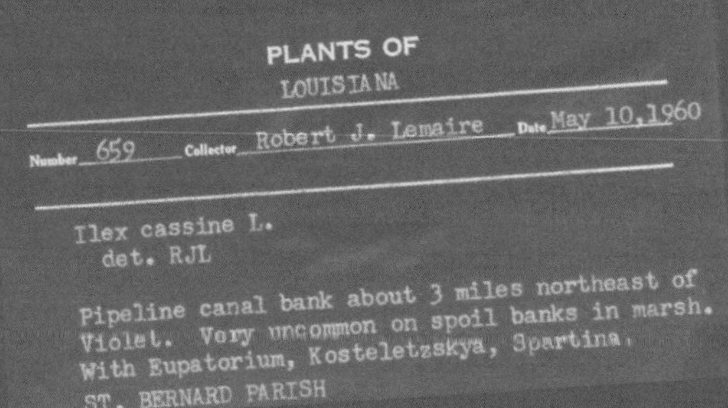

PLANTS OF
LOUISIANA

Number 659   Collector Robert J. Lemaire   Date May 10, 1960

Ilex cassine L.
det. RJL

Pipeline canal bank about 3 miles northeast of
Violet. Very uncommon on spoil banks in marsh.
With Eupatorium, Kosteletzskya, Spartina.
ST. BERNARD PARISH

SI-3198f
3-7-79

PLANTS of   NEW YORK
Orleans County

Prunus virginiana L. Det. H Wells
12 Aug 1996

Locality   Troutburg, south shore of Lake
Ontario.

Occurrence   At top of narrow pebble beach.

Date   May 29, 1979   Alt.   m

Coll. F.R. Fosberg   No.   59072

Remarks   Shrub 3 m tall, flowers white,
fragrant.

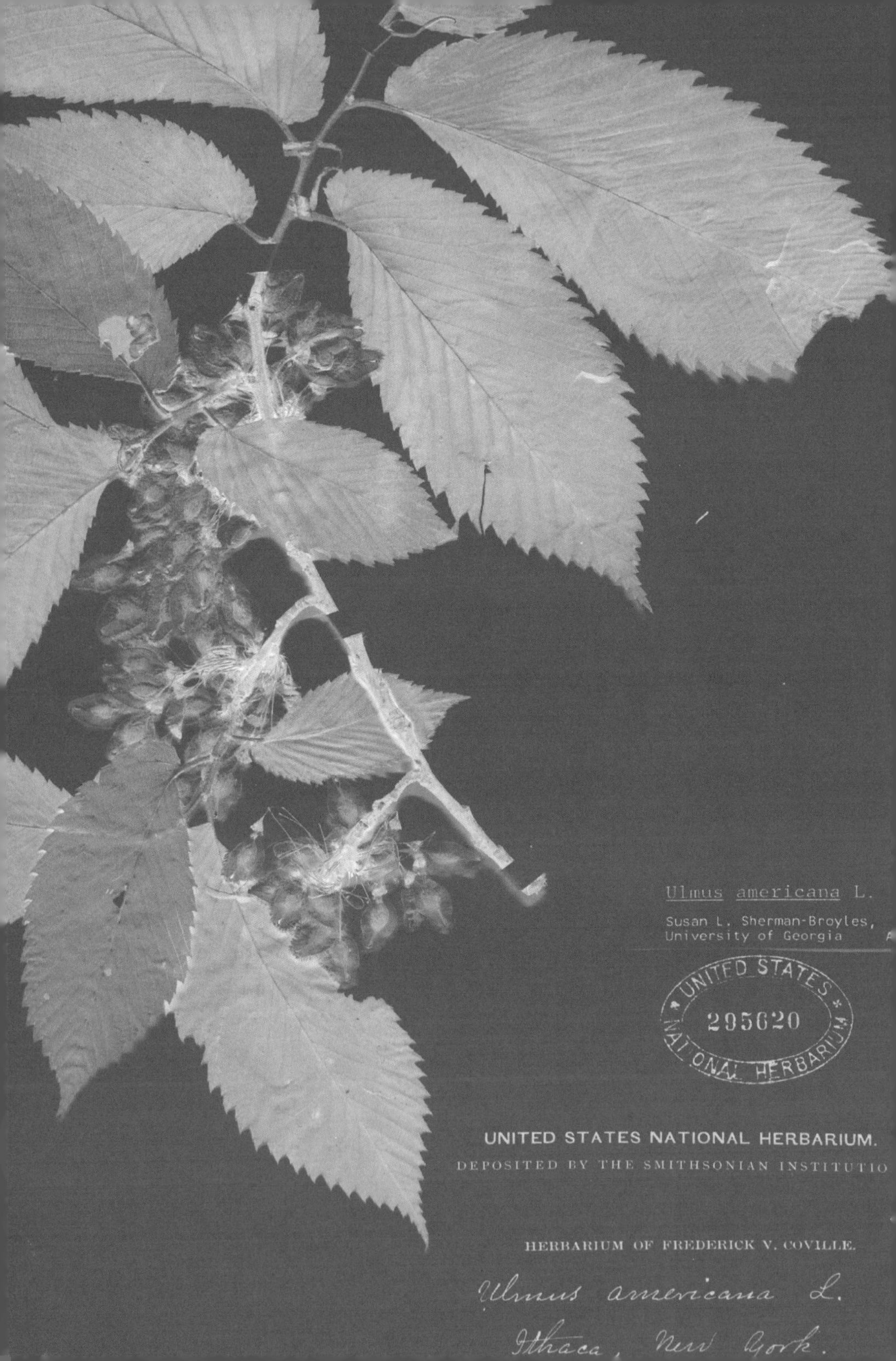

Ulmus americana L.
Susan L. Sherman-Broyles,
University of Georgia
UNITED STATES
295620
NATIONAL HERBARIUM
UNITED STATES NATIONAL HERBARIUM.
DEPOSITED BY THE SMITHSONIAN INSTITUTION
HERBARIUM OF FREDERICK V. COVILLE.
Ulmus americana L.
Ithaca, New York.